Create Big Romance
on a $mall Budget

Tired of the usual dinner-and-a-movie dates? Looking for new ways to connect with your spouse?

Energize your marriage by getting out of your normal routine with the help of these 52 creative date ideas. From outdoor dates to out-on-the-town dates, you and your spouse will have no trouble finding the perfect date that fits your mood—all on a $10 budget!

See for yourself how new experiences can help you bond together and nurture your relationship. Which of these will be the first of your Great Dates?

- TIME TRAVEL GREAT DATE
- MOONLIGHT/SUNRISE GREAT DATE
- BUCKET LIST GREAT DATE
- SURPRISE ME! GREAT DATE

Each date includes easy preparation suggestions, tips for the date, talking points to enhance your conversations, and a Great Date takeaway. What are you waiting for?

Peter and Heather Larson and **David and Claudia Arp** help couples of all ages and stages build great marriages. Peter is a licensed clinical psychologist and Heather is a Christian relationship coach. David and Claudia, founders of Marriage Alive, created the many 10 Great Dates® seminars and resources now popular across the U.S. and internationally.

BETHANYHOUSE
a division of Baker Publishing Group

$10
GREAT
DATES

Other Resources From David & Claudia Arp

10 Great Dates to Energize Your Marriage
(book/DVD curriculum)

10 Great Dates Before You Say "I Do" (book/DVD curriculum)

10 Great Dates for Empty Nesters

52 Fantastic Dates for You and Your Mate

The Second Half of Marriage (book/DVD curriculum)

Answering the 8 Cries of the Spirited Child

Fighting for Your Empty Nest Marriage (with Scott Stanley, Howard Markman, and Susan Blumberg)

Loving Your Relatives

The Connected Family

No Time for Sex

Suddenly They're 13!

Other Resources From Peter & Heather Larson

10 Great Dates: Connecting Faith, Love & Marriage (with David and Claudia Arp)

The Couple Checkup (with David H. Olson and Amy Olson-Sigg)

10 Great Dates Before You Say "I Do" (DVD curriculum)

Great Dates Connect (DVD curriculum)

PREPARE to Last (DVD curriculum with David H. Olson and Jeff & Debbie McElroy)

PREPARE/ENRICH: Customized Version (inventory/ assessment with David H. Olson)

Couple Checkup (inventory/assessment with David H. Olson)

$10 GREAT DTES

Connecting Love, Marriage,
and Fun on a Budget

PETER & HEATHER
LARSON

AND

DAVID & CLAUDIA
ARP

BETHANY HOUSE PUBLISHERS
a division of Baker Publishing Group
Minneapolis, Minnesota

© 2014 by Peter Larson, Heather Larson, David Arp, and Claudia Arp

Published by Bethany House Publishers
11400 Hampshire Avenue South
Bloomington, Minnesota 55438
www.bethanyhouse.com

Bethany House Publishers is a division of
Baker Publishing Group, Grand Rapids, Michigan

Printed in the United States of America

Library of Congress Cataloging-in-Publication Data is on file at the Library of Congress, Washington, DC.

ISBN 978-0-7642-1135-5 (pbk.)

Unless otherwise indicated, Scripture quotations are from the Holy Bible, New International Version®. NIV®. Copyright © 1973, 1978, 1984, 2011 by Biblica, Inc.™ Used by permission of Zondervan. All rights reserved worldwide. www.zondervan.com.

Scripture quotations identified ESV are from The Holy Bible, English Standard Version® (ESV®), copyright © 2001 by Crossway, a publishing ministry of Good News Publishers. Used by permission. All rights reserved. ESV Text Edition: 2007.

Scripture quotations identified NLT are from the Holy Bible, New Living Translation, copyright © 1996, 2004, 2007 by Tyndale House Foundation. Used by permission of Tyndale House Publishers, Inc., Carol Stream, Illinois 60188. All rights reserved.

Cover design by Greg Jackson, Thinkpen Design, Inc.

Authors are represented by WordServe Literary Group.

14   15   16   17   18   19   7   6   5   4   3   2   1

To couples everywhere
who want to add fun to their marriage
through Great Dates

Contents

Introduction   11

Adventure Great Dates

1. Out-of-Towners Great Date   17
2. Gifts on a Budget Great Date   20
3. Workshop Great Date   23
4. Yellow Brick Road Great Date   26
5. Home Improvement Great Date   29

Out-on-the-Town Great Dates

6. Just Desserts Great Date   35
7. Card Shop Great Date   38
8. Parade of Homes Great Date   41
9. Library Great Date   44
10. Photo Great Date   47
11. Breakfast Great Date   50
12. Running Errands Great Date   53
13. Night at the Museum Great Date   56

At-Home Great Dates

14. Time Travel Great Date   61
15. Beating the Blahs Great Date   64
16. Game Night Great Date   67

Contents

17. Coupon Great Date 70
18. Create in the Kitchen Great Date 73
19. Wedding Video Great Date 76

The Great Outdoors Great Dates
20. Take a Hike (Together) Great Date 81
21. Light the Fire Great Date 84
22. Movie on Location Great Date 87
23. Little League Great Date 90
24. Find Our Pace Great Date 93
25. Playground Great Date 96
26. Moonlight/Sunrise Great Date 99

Marriage Pick-Me-Up Great Dates
27. Family Tree Great Date 105
28. Drive-Through Great Date 108
29. Marriage Checkup Great Date 111
30. Volunteer Great Date 114
31. Bucket List Great Date 117
32. Gratitude Great Date 120

Romantic Great Dates
33. Dining Under the Stars Great Date 125
34. At-Home Spa Great Date 129
35. Let's Rumba Great Date 132
36. Three Wishes Great Date 134
37. Hotel Lobby Great Date 137
38. Surprise Me! Great Date 140

Seasonal Specials Great Dates
39. Spring Festival Great Date 145
40. Green Thumb Great Date 148

Contents

41. Fun in the Water Great Date   151

42. Farmers Market Great Date   154

43. Apple Picking Great Date   157

44. Snow Hike Great Date   159

45. Holiday Workout Great Date   161

46. Christmas Lights Great Date   164

Unique and Unusual Great Dates

47. Solid Gold Great Date   168

48. Romantic Dinner at Nine Great Date   171

49. Take a Spin Great Date   174

50. Play With a Pet Great Date   177

51. A River Runs Through It Great Date   180

52. Estate Sale Great Date   183

Cheap Child Care Options   187

Acknowledgments   189

Notes   190

About the Authors   191

Introduction

A recent conversation:

Question: "What's your favorite date?"

Answer: "You mean before we were married?"

Question: "No, what's your favorite date from the past couple of months?"

Answer: [Silence, then . . .] "We don't actually date. We're so busy, and it's super expensive! It's just not easy to do."

If you can identify with this conversation, or if you're simply looking for ways to energize your relationship, we've got you covered. In the following pages we offer 52 Great Dates that are easy to pull off, easy to do (lots of tips and helps), and best of all, doable on a budget of $10 or less!

Think back to your initial dating days and why you dated each other in the first place. When we ask dating couples (the unmarried type) why they date, we hear comments like *"Because I'm crazy about her." "He makes me happy." "I want our relationship to grow." "I want to know her on a deeper level." "We're really attracted to each other."* Wouldn't it be great if married couples could tap into this same positive energy in an ongoing way? Dating on a regular basis is a fun way for couples to rejuvenate their love for each other.

We (the Arps) often say, "Fun in marriage is serious business!" Think about it: have you ever met a couple on the way to the divorce

11

court who were having fun together? Don't think so! And how do you put more fun in your relationship? One way is by having regular date nights. Dates with a purpose. (Not just dinner and a movie.) Research reveals that dating can make a positive difference in a relationship. But here's the catch: predictable dinner-and-a-movie dates have less impact than dates that stretch you and take you out of your normal routine. New experiences help you bond together and often result in a big payoff for your marriage. But one of you needs to take the initiative!

Taking time and effort to initiate a date sends several powerful messages to your spouse. It communicates that you want to be together and that your spouse is worth the time, money, and effort involved. Most couples complain about overscheduled lives, so taking time for a date shows that you want to give your significant other your attention. With so many things competing for our time, dates rarely just happen naturally. A date communicates, "I choose you as a priority, and I want to be intentional about nurturing our relationship."

We (the Larsons) can tell when it has been too long since we've been on a date. We begin to feel disconnected, and we function more like roommates than spouses. We become short with each other in the midst of our schedules, kids, and responsibilities. This general sense of distance and tension is a signal that we need time alone as a couple, time to reconnect. Maybe you can identify with us.

So, what makes a date great? No rules exist for what constitutes a successful date, but there are several common elements: quality time together, giving each of you a break from your normal routine, a shared activity, and conversation. Men tend to relax through doing an activity; women often relax by talking. So if your date includes both an activity and the opportunity to talk, you're on your way to a great date.

In the following pages, we offer you a variety of fun dates that include the above elements and will take you out of your norm. Unlike books you read from cover to cover, you can read this book spontaneously. Our dates are divided into eight sections, each offering a

different type of date. Simply read the section that fits your mood, then choose your next Great Date from that section. (All dates should fit your $10 budget!) You'll find everything from Romantic Dates to The Great Outdoors Dates to Out-on-the-Town Dates.

With each date, you will find your own personal dating guide with *Before Your Date* suggestions as well as tips for your actual date in the *On Your Date* section. We've included *Talking Points* that can be conversation starters and enhancers. And for each date we offer a *Great Date Takeaway*—a thought to ponder and apply to your relationship. While most of the dates are fun and easy to pull off, some dates will take you deeper. Others require more energy and effort. Not all dates will appeal to you, so we give you permission to pick and choose what sounds fun to both of you.

We hope our dates will result in an experience of enjoyment and improved connection. Hopefully, they will lead to many meaningful conversations and enhance your communication, flexibility, and general sense of relational well-being. Now it's time to make your marriage come alive with fun, laughter, and good times together! Enjoy your Great Dates!

At some point in your dating adventures, we'd love to hear about your favorite fun and economical Great Date. You can reach us at www.facebook.com/10GreatDates or www.10greatdates.org, where you'll also find more tips to energize your marriage, as well as information about other dating resources.

Adventure
GREAT DATES

Out-of-Towners
Great Date

Recently Claudia and I (Dave) had houseguests, and, of course, living in the Washington, D.C., area, at the top of the agenda was seeing the sights. While we have lived here for a number of years, we always get a different perspective when we look at our hometown through the eyes of a tourist.

The Idea

On this date, you can be the "out-of-towners" and look at your own town through a tourist filter. Pretend this is your first visit. You may be amazed what you discover about your own stomping grounds and how fortunate you are to live so close to so many interesting sights.

Before Your Date

- Research your local area and discover fun things to do and free venues of interest.
- Search the web to find discount days, coupons, and other deals for the places you plan to visit.

- Contact the chamber of commerce for free brochures and maps of the area.

- If you live in a small town, you might want to include a broader area for your "tourist" date.

- If you need child care, check out the Cheap Child Care Options near the back of this book.

On Your Date

- Allow plenty of time for your date. Remember that you are "tourists" seeing the sights for the first time.

- Consider taking your own walking tour of the downtown area. You get a different perspective when you're walking vs. driving.

- Wear comfortable clothes and shoes.

- You might want to wear a backpack and bring along water and snacks to help stay on budget.

- Be sure to have a camera or smartphone to document your date. A small flexible tripod will facilitate taking fun couple pictures, or if it's an option, reverse the camera on your smartphone, stretch out your arm, and snap a selfie of both of you.

Talking Points

- How does putting on "tourist glasses" change your perspective?

- How willing are you to venture out and try new things?

- What did you learn about your hometown that you didn't know before this date?

- If you were giving a guided tour, what points of interest would you include?

- What other sights would you like to visit on another date?

Great Date Takeaway

When we take the time to explore together, we gain a new appreciation of where we live, work, and play. How does this relate to your relationship? Even the ordinary and familiar can seem different when looked at through the eyes of an out-of-towner. What are the great things about your relationship that others might notice but perhaps you overlook? It's time to celebrate some of the positive attractions in your own "hometown" marriage.

2

Gifts on a Budget
Great Date

Heather is a natural spender and loves to give gifts to others. We like to say she's good for the economy—the money comes in and the money goes out. I'm a natural-born saver (Peter), so the budget part of this date speaks my language. At times, our different financial personalities have led to tension, and I know we are not alone in this. The key is finding a balance between savings, spending, and giving. On this date, you'll have the opportunity to find that balance as you give the gift of something special for your spouse *on a $5 budget*.

The Idea

Together head to the local mall or department store with the task of buying each other a gift. The challenge is to spend just $5 on each gift. Yes, this includes tax! You get to practice staying within a budget. You also get to surprise each other with a thoughtful gift.

Before Your Date

- Find child care if you need it.

- Choose a store with a wide range of inexpensive merchandise or a mall with several stores.

- Make sure you each have just $5 cash to spend on each gift. (Remember, you're practicing staying on budget.)

On Your Date

- First, set a time and location you'll meet together once you're done. Then split up and shop separately for about fifteen to twenty minutes. You may need longer to find a meaningful bargain!

- Try to find something special or significant for your partner. It doesn't need to be big or expensive to be meaningful. For example, Heather loves the candy Hot Tamales. Every time I buy her some, she feels loved because it shows I was thinking of her.

- Hit the sale racks and check out counters where stores often have discounted impulse buys.

- For the big exchange, consider heading to a location where you'll have time and space to talk privately.

Talking Points

- Was it more fun to give or receive the gift?

- What did you wish you could buy, but had to pass up due to the price?

- Were you able to stay under budget? If not, explain what happened.

- Why do you think budgets are so challenging to establish and keep?

Great Date Takeaway

This date provides several opportunities. First, you can have fun giving and receiving a gift. Second, you have the opportunity to resist going over budget. Every store is filled with items that cost more than your $5 budget, and you'll need to resist the temptation to go overboard. Spending some money can be fun and lead to great experiences and memories, but overspending can create stress that leads to challenges. Think about some strategies to keep your household budget on track. If you don't have a budget, consider creating one today.

3

Workshop
Great Date

You may have hidden dating resources right in your own community. Free seminars and workshops provide not only fun dates but also helpful information. Recently we (the Arps) attended a free two-hour workshop at a local garden center. The topic was how to prune and maintain your shrubs and trees. As we listened to the garden specialist share valuable tips, we sipped our free coffee and enjoyed free muffins. (This also doubled as a Breakfast Great Date.) Each attendee received a 15-percent-off coupon, which meant with our $10 budget we could go home with at least one new plant. But wait—that's not all! This is a date that keeps giving. Later that week we had a Green Thumb Great Date, where in our own garden we practiced what we learned about pruning plants and also planted our new fern by our dry streambed. (See A River Runs Through It Great Date.)

The Idea

You can turn free community workshops and seminars into great dates. Also, many gardening centers, home improvement stores, and other retailers offer free classes and workshops. You can learn not only how to garden but also how to wallpaper a room or tile

your bathroom. Choose a learning opportunity that sounds interesting to both of you, and you'll have a great date while gaining valuable information.

Before Your Date

- Research your local area to find fun, free workshops on topics of interest.

- Topics might include gardening, organizing your closets, or the history of your local area. Google your zip code for free workshops and see what you uncover. In our area, opportunities included free computer classes, seminars on healthy living, the arts and literature, and budgeting.

- Together, choose a topic from the list you have made and plan your date! As in our case, this date may lead to other dates as you apply what you will learn about your chosen topic.

- Check ahead to see if coffee and refreshments will be served.

On Your Date

- Many free workshops promote paid services. Go with your willpower in place. Agree together that you will not sign up for a service or commit yourself financially until you've had time to explore all the ramifications. Ignoring this advice can result in pushing your date way over budget!

- Because there are two of you, your spouse may be more interested in the chosen topic than you are. If so, give a gift of love. The next time, you can pick the topic.

Talking Points

- How did you become interested in this topic?
- What new insights did you gain?

- How will this new knowledge help you?
- What other topics would be on the top of your list to pursue?

Great Date Takeaway

In marriage, as in life, you will have opportunities to grow and strengthen your relationship. But growth opportunities may not be obvious. You need to be intentional and seek them out. Growth requires effort. A relationship that is growing is moving forward. Standing still is not an option. In the rapids of life, you'll either be pushing upstream or floating downstream. Choose to row upstream together; keep learning new skills and build a great marriage.

4

Yellow Brick Road
Great Date

Let your sense of adventure lead you on a Yellow Brick Road Great
Date. We (the Arps) chose yellow because that's the color of the
back roads on our local map. It all started during a drive home
from visiting with Claudia's mom. The night was dark, and without
planning a Yellow Brick Road Date, we ended up having one. It
became more interesting when the yellow brick road turned into a
gravel road, or as Claudia described it, a gravel *path*. We had radio
reception, so we knew we were near civilization—we just didn't
know how to get there! Finally, we turned around (something I
absolutely hate to do) and eventually found our way back to the
beaten path we recognized. We still talk about our Yellow Brick
Road Date in the North Georgia mountains.

The Idea

The idea is to discover the back roads that you aren't familiar with.
You might want to pick a twenty-five- or thirty-mile radius and
see what you can discover. The distance you can go on your $10
budget depends on what you have to pay for gas and what kind
of gas mileage you get. However far you go, it's fun to see what
you can discover.

Before Your Date

- Pick an area you both want to explore.

- Decide how much time (and gas) you have for your date. This will help you decide how far you'll go. (Remember, you'll need gas for the return trip too!)

- You might want to use an old-fashioned map (folds and all), or you can print a map from the Internet or use a map app.

- Pack a picnic lunch or dinner, as well as water and snacks you can eat along the way.

On Your Date

- Venture out and take the back roads. Avoid interstates and four-lane highways.

- Pass up fast-food or chain restaurants.

- Stop at any interesting place you find. You'll be amazed at what you discover. We've found everything from woolly worm races to great antiques shops.

- Sometimes we even get out of the car, sit on a rock or log, or take a short walk and enjoy the great outdoors.

Talking Points

- What did you discover in your own geographical area?

- What surprised you the most?

- Can you think of roads in your life that have taken unpredictable turns?

- Talk about what you appreciate about being on the same road together.

- In what ways can you make your life a little less predictable?

Great Date Takeaway

When you get in a rut, life becomes too predictable. The Yellow Brick Road Date took you off the beaten paths you are so familiar with and gave you a new, fun experience. Likewise, you need to find new and interesting ways to refresh your relationship—maybe even venturing out and signing up for a marriage workshop, seminar, or retreat. Thank God that each day offers you a fresh adventure together.

5

Home Improvement
Great Date

When you get the urge to spruce up your living quarters, why not book a home improvement dream date? It doesn't matter that you have no money for remodeling that outdated kitchen or transforming the deck into a year-round sun-room with removable windows. Not to worry. Or perhaps you are still renting and dreaming about future home ownership. Not a problem. You can enjoy a Home Improvement Great Date right now.

The Idea

The suggested setting for this date is any local home improvement store, such as Home Depot or Lowe's. Since you're only dreaming, you don't need a big wad of money. You can leave your credit cards at home. This date can be relaxing, inexpensive, and fun, and may pay off in the future. Maybe one day you will buy a fixer-upper home, and you'll be ahead of the game with a file of great ideas.

Before Your Date

- Talk beforehand about what future home improvement projects might be on your dream list.

- You may want to choose a couple of areas to concentrate on, such as a kitchen upgrade or bathroom remodel.

- Before your date, you might want to measure and take pictures of the area you want to update. This will help you plan and budget for the materials you'll need.

- You can also go with a blank slate and look at all the displays for ideas for future projects.

On Your Date

- To keep this date on budget, resist impulse buying!
- Take along a pen and small notebook to jot down ideas.
- Take pictures with your phone or camera of things you like.
- When you return home, you might want to catalog your date by writing down your ideas and putting them in a file for future reference.
- Consider starting a home improvement savings account!

Talking Points

As you explore potential home improvement projects, you will discover more about your individual likes and dislikes. Take turns answering questions, such as:

- What is your favorite color?
- What style of furniture would you choose if money were no object?
- If you could live anywhere in the world, where would you live?
- What design of house would you pick?
- What is your favorite place or room in your home?
- Where in your home do the best "couple times" happen?

Great Date Takeaway

When it comes to home improvement dreams, how many likes do you have in common? Did some of your differences surprise you? In any relationship there is some give and take. That's all good unless one is doing most of the giving and the other most of the taking. An important relationship skill is the ability to work through differences, to compromise, and to complement each other in the ways you are different. God made each person unique—no two alike—but our diversity can be grounds for a great relationship! And your future home might be even more charming than if you both thought alike.

Out-on-the-Town
GREAT DATES

6

Just Desserts
Great Date

When Peter and I (Heather) were poor graduate students, we discovered a great way to get out and enjoy an evening on the town without dropping $100! We enjoyed going to an area called Old Town in Pasadena, California. There we could walk outdoors, window shop, visit a gallery, and take in some great people-watching. We had fun trying different restaurants all over town. By just having dessert, we could stay on budget and still enjoy places where we might not be able to afford a full dinner.

The Idea

Officially, the phrase is spelled *just deserts,* referring to a reward or punishment that is deserved. Our Just Desserts Date simply makes sure the reward is always tasty and inexpensive. By eating your main course at home, a Just Desserts Date provides the experience of a fancy night out while staying on budget. Often women enjoy getting dressed up and heading out on a date. I know I do! I love picking out the outfit, doing my hair, and then going out for something special. However, having an elegant dinner out gets expensive—*quickly*. Just dessert at a fancy restaurant can be an excuse for a special outing together.

Before Your Date

- Eat dinner at home.

- Dress up for your date. Wear something you know your spouse will appreciate too.

- Plan where to go that will allow you to extend your evening together beyond dessert.

- If needed, make arrangements for your kids while you are out. (See Cheap Child Care Options near the back of this book.)

On Your Date

- Try someplace new or somewhere you might not usually go because of the price. After all, you can always split a dessert for under $10!

- Remember to arrive after the regular dinner rush, and tip your server well.

- Eat slowly so your dessert lasts and you get a chance to enjoy the atmosphere and food.

Talking Points

- What is your favorite dessert ever?

- If money were no object, where would you go for a five-course dinner?

- Tell your spouse three things that you think are "sweet" about him or her.

- Talk about what you are thankful for in your lives, and start a gratitude list.

Great Date Takeaway

Dessert is all about the overflow of sweets. Take this time to reflect together about all of the blessings or "sweet things" in your marriage. You may be in a tough spot in life: perhaps you're trying to keep up with young kids, facing financial stress, or dealing with a health challenge. Whatever the circumstances, there are still things we can be thankful for. After your date, you can take your gratitude list home and find a place where you can look at it and add to it as you think of more positives. You may challenge yourselves to add one new thing each day for a week. Focusing on the "sweet spots" in your life can give you a renewed perspective on whatever trials you may be facing.

7

Card Shop
Great Date

In our world of Twitter, Instagram, Facebook, and who knows what else will be in vogue before this book's first printing is dry, it's a treat to get something printed or handwritten from the one we love. So here is a fun date you might want to try—especially if you have a favorite card shop nearby.

The Idea

You can give each other lovely expensive cards, and it doesn't have to cost you a penny. Dave and I (Claudia) had our first (unplanned) Card Shop Date several years ago in San Francisco. We were in town to lead a Valentine's Day seminar the next day and had a couple of hours to kill before meeting friends for dinner. Admiring the shops as we walked through the streets, we found a cute card shop. Realizing neither of us had gotten a Valentine's card for the other, we went into the shop and inaugurated our first Card Shop Date, which we have repeated many times since that day. Individually, we look through the cards, and when we find ones we really like, we give them to each other. After reading them, we simply put them back! This makes for a really cheap date!

Before Your Date

- This date requires little preparation. Actually, you can have a spontaneous card date anytime you're in a grocery store with a card section, a store such as Target or Walmart, or even your local pharmacy.

- Another great place for a Card Shop Date is a bookstore that has a coffee shop. You can share cards with each other and then use your $10 budget for a café latte (or another favorite drink).

On Your Date

- Be extravagant. You aren't limited to just one or two cards. And you don't have to be concerned about the price of the card, since you are going to put it back.

- A fundamental rule for this date is to be sure to put the card back where you got it! (This pleases the card shop owner.)

- If you find cards you really love, splurge and buy one for each other. You could keep it until sometime when you feel your partner needs a bit of encouragement. He or she will probably have forgotten all about your Card Shop Date, and it might be just the pickup needed.

- For the super creative: Skip the card shop and make your own cards. Or let your time in the card shop inspire you to design your own cards for each other.

Talking Points

- What was your favorite card?
- What are five words you might use if you were designing your own card for your spouse?
- How important is the written word to you?
- On what occasions would it be fun to get a card from your spouse?

- What about this experience has been encouraging to you?
- What are other ways you might like to be encouraged in the future?

Great Date Takeaway

Everyone needs encouragement. Whether you're going through a hard time or not, it can make such a difference to know that someone loves you and expresses that love through actions, words, and something as simple as a card or note. The apostle Paul encouraged the Philippians to have positive thoughts—to think about whatever is true, noble, right, pure, lovely, and admirable.[1] Good advice for us today! Did you realize that it takes five positive statements to offset one negative statement? A Card Shop Date is an easy and fun way to up those positives in a very short time.

Parade of Homes
Great Date

Whether you are a homeowner or you dream about having your own home someday, here is a date that might just be up your alley. For years Dave and I (Claudia) have enjoyed going to open houses and remodeling shows, and sometimes just walking through building supply stores and getting ideas for home improvements. If you are fortunate enough to have yearly Parade of Homes events in your area, all the better. When we lived in Knoxville, Tennessee, we could purchase one entry to tour new homes in several different communities, and we stretched our Parade of Homes Date into multiple dates. Sometimes the theme was starter homes, other times it was more upscale homes. We always looked for what we liked, what we didn't like, and what we could adapt or do in the future to our own home.

The Idea

Attend the Parade of Homes event in your area and enjoy walking through newly built homes with all the latest trends. You can also look for open houses for homes on the market. Often homes are "staged to sell," so you can get tips for the future should you find yourself making a transition and needing to sell your home.

Another variation would be attending remodeling shows. Here in the Washington, D.C., area, we have several each year and they can be great fun. Often they offer free seminars for everything from decorative paint finishes to adding curb appeal. We come home with free reusable bags, yardsticks, and other free gadgets, plus lots of good ideas.

Before Your Date

- Do your research. What's coming up in your area?
- Take water and snacks along.
- Take your camera or smartphone and a note pad to jot down ideas.
- Decide which homes you want to be sure to preview.

On Your Date

- Wear comfortable clothing and shoes, and be prepared to walk and walk and walk—but trust us, it's worth it!
- Allow plenty of time and pace yourself.
- Take pictures of what you like. If you have one area or room in your home that you are interested in updating, you might want to measure it or take a picture before you go.
- This is a great opportunity to ask the experts any questions you might have.
- Collect brochures and contact information. When you get home, you can go through them and keep the ones you both like for your "dream file."

Talking Points

- What would your ideal home look like?
- What features in a home do you both like and feel are important? What features do you agree you could do without?
- How does your home reflect your values?
- If you were downsizing, what would your home/condo/apartment look like?
- What are the essentials?
- What could you do without?

Great Date Takeaway

Building a house is similar to building a marriage. Our mentors, Drs. David and Vera Mace, often shared this analogy: your wedding day can be compared to a vacant lot with building materials but no structure. Your wedding was a lovely event, but it is not a marriage. Your marriage is what you build over the years. What are the foundational principles upon which your marriage is being built? A wise proverb reminds us that *a house is built by wisdom, and through understanding it is established.*[2] How are you doing at understanding each other and building your marriage?

9

Library
Great Date

In today's world of instant downloads of books, movies, and music, it's easy to forget the treasures public libraries hold. On this date you can discover some of them.

The Idea

When Peter and I (Heather) lived near Pasadena, California, one of our favorite dates was going to the Pasadena Central Library, which was built in 1927 and is on the National Register of Historic Places. The dark wood and quiet halls created a beautiful setting for our library dates. On this date, take a break from the screens in your life and visit a public library. Today, libraries house a lot more resources than traditional books. You can also check out books or music on CDs or DVDs that may not be available from other sources. You might find an old classic film or documentary. Have fun and see what you can discover together. You just might be surprised at what you find on your Library Date.

Before Your Date

- Search the web for libraries in your area and choose the one you want to visit on your date.

- If you live in a city with a library that you already frequent, consider visiting a new library.

- Make a list of resources and topics to check out on your date, such as books on travel, hobbies, parenting, cookbooks, home improvement projects, or relationships.

- Check out the bestseller list in the newspaper or online and see what piques your interest.

On Your Date

- Explore the library together. Observe the architecture and layout of the library. Are there comfortable chairs where you can sit and browse through books and magazines together?

- Sign up for a library card if you don't already have one.

- Check out different areas, such as the travel section to learn about foreign places you'd like to visit someday, or a home project, craft, or hobby you might be interested in exploring together.

- What exercise and healthy-living resources can you find?

- If you have children, look for some parenting resources and tips at the library.

- We can all do more research to strengthen our marriages. What books can you find that will be a new source of encouragement?

- Extend your library date by checking out a book, CD, and/or DVD to take home with you. Plan a time to read with, or to, each other. You can both unwind while you listen to a book on a CD.

Talking Points

- What did you discover together at the library?
- Were there any surprises?
- Learning together can be inspiring! What subjects might you like to learn more about?
- What are two or three of the best books you've ever read? What made them great?
- What's at the top of your reading list?

Great Date Takeaway

How well do you know your spouse? Can you "read" him or her like a book? We've found there is always something new we can learn about each other. It would be easy for me to think, *Oh, I've been married for twenty years. I know everything there is to know about Peter.* But this is a slippery slope. When you stop studying your spouse, you stop being curious about who they are and who they are becoming, and you run the risk of growing apart. None of us wants to wake up one morning to discover that we no longer know each other. Be willing to keep learning—always curious, always growing, and always booking more dates!

10

Photo
Great Date

When was the last time you took a photo of just the two of you? Often we are the ones taking the pictures of others. Turn the camera around, find some great photo locations, and snap away!

The Idea

One couple we know celebrated their first anniversary by having a photo date. The husband knew his wife loved pictures and photo albums, so he asked her to get ready to have some pictures taken and then took her on a photo date. They drove to places significant to their relationship, starting with the restaurant they visited on their first date. He then stopped at several locations relevant to their dating history and took more photos together. Their final destination was the church where they were married. Later, he put the photos together into an album for her. You don't have to wait for an anniversary or special occasion. You can have a Photo Date today!

Before Your Date

- Choose a location, or locations, you would like to go on your date. You may consider places popular for photo shoots, or you may choose to photograph locations that are meaningful to your relationship.

- Decide what to wear. You don't need to dress up, but be sure to choose what will look good in the pictures. Pick colors that complement each other and patterns that aren't too busy. If these are to be candid shots, you will want to be comfortable and casual.

- Be sure your camera is charged, or bring fresh batteries if needed.

On Your Date

- Take your camera or smartphone and head out to some scenic location.

- Snap shots of each other and shots together as a couple. If someone comes by, you could ask him or her to take the photo of the two of you.

- Be creative about your poses. You may want a picture of a kiss!

- Be willing to be silly and laugh at yourselves. With digital photography, it is easy to delete the photos you don't like.

- Take pictures in several locations. You could have a theme of historical locations in your community, where you could take pictures of yourselves with historical backdrops. You may drive around town and snap photos in front of your favorite restaurants or other places significant to your relationship.

- Print your photos at home or use an online printing site. Put the prints together in a memory book. Life is short. Take time to capture an evening in your lives together. The memory will provide laughter and joy for years to come, both for you and other family members.

Talking Points

- When was the last time you took photos as a couple?
- What was the first picture taken of the two of you? Can you find a copy?
- What is your favorite picture taken together?
- Of all the photos you took while on your date, which was your favorite?
- A photo is an image from one moment in time. What are some of your favorite images or memories of your relationship?

Great Date Takeaway

Taking the time for a Photo Date will give you an opportunity to capture a time in your marriage that you can look back on and remember fondly someday. What will you remember from this time in your lives? What are some of the things that seem important or consuming now that you suspect will not be as significant in the future? I think back to the days when potty training our three children was all-consuming and a constant struggle. Now I can remember that season with a smile! Looking back gives us perspective that today's challenges will not be forever. Remembering God's faithfulness in the past can give strength for today and hope for tomorrow.

Breakfast
Great Date

Eating out for dinner can quickly become expensive. Treating your-selves to a lunch or breakfast out is a less expensive option and a break from the typical date night.

The Idea

With the hectic pace of life these days, many feel tired by dinnertime or feel the need to vent at home about a busy day. This gets in the way of relaxing with each other. In the morning, however, you are fresh and ready to spend quality time together.

One couple we know has a weekly breakfast date. As newly-weds, they needed to find a date on a budget, and breakfast was the least expensive meal. They found a restaurant with a $2 stack of pancakes, and that became their place! When moving to a different location, they enjoyed several dates before they discovered their favorite breakfast place. Now when they go to *their* restaurant on Friday mornings, their waitress knows them by name! They have a special table, and their coffee comes quickly. They love the consistency that this weekly date brings to their marriage. On busy weekdays, they know they can look forward to connecting again each Friday morning. You could also turn this into an at-home date.

If the kids are off at school, bring the breakfast treats back home. Enjoy breakfast in bed together. Now, that's romantic!

Before Your Date

- Find a morning that both of you can get some time away together.
- Choose a breakfast restaurant. You can find inexpensive breakfast options at coffee shops, bakeries, or bagel restaurants.
- You could even turn your breakfast date into a picnic or an at-home date by picking up rolls and fruit from a nearby grocery store.

On Your Date

- Be creative. Consider ordering one large breakfast to split. Often there is more than enough food for both of you.
- Skip the juice, as it is often an extra cost that can add up quickly.
- We (Peter and Heather) love gourmet coffee drinks, but they can be expensive. We have found that ordering a single large latte and then sharing it in two cups is less expensive than ordering two smaller coffees.

Talking Points

- Which one of you is more of a morning person?
- When do you feel the most rested and relaxed? How long has it been since you've felt that way?
- Every morning ushers in a fresh new day. What can you be hopeful for today?
- Is there anything weighing you down that you could let go of today?

Great Date Takeaway

Morning is a time for a fresh start. An individual who holds on to past regrets or disappointments becomes burdened, and this can take a toll on your relationships as well. You may have heard, "Do not let the sun go down while you are still angry."[3] There is wisdom in letting the past stay in the past and choosing to start fresh today. There is a difference between simply ignoring something from the past and choosing to let it go. Letting it go will be a way to leave it behind, so whatever disappointment, hurt, or anger you experienced is no longer your burden to carry. What can you let go of today in order to give yourself and your marriage a fresh new start?

12

Running Errands
Great Date

Life can be so hectic. Reading a book like this, with so many date ideas, can feel like a far-fetched fantasy. You may find yourself asking, "Who has time for so many dates?" Between work, home, and kids, schedules can become overwhelmingly full. Rather than fighting this fact, why not look for ways to multitask together by having an errand date? Start by acknowledging your busy life and giving yourself permission to connect while covering your bases. Putting a "dating spin" on running errands together can actually transform work into fun. Think back to your initial dating days. When Heather and I (Peter) were dating, it seemed any opportunity to be together became a chance to be on a date. Running to the home improvement store or going to the grocery store became a date. One of our early dates involved hanging out together while she got the oil changed in her car!

The Idea

Make your list of errands and things you need to get done, then head out and begin checking things off your list. Along the way, take twenty or thirty minutes for a sit-down face-to-face discussion. It could be that you simply have a cup of coffee, or share

a treat together. (The money you spend on your list of errands doesn't count toward your date because you were going to spend that anyway.) Your only expense will be the money you choose to spend on coffee or snacks.

Before Your Date

- Make your shopping list together and plan your route.
- If needed, arrange your child care.

On Your Date

- Play some of your favorite music in the car.
- Stay positive and try to be present with one another. Don't let your to-do list overshadow the chance to have a conversation.

Talking Points

- What are you feeling good about these days?
- What is causing you stress?
- How can you help each other better manage the busyness and stress of life?
- What in your weekly schedules could you change or reprioritize to free up more time?
- Schedule your next date and commit to protecting that time.

Great Date Takeaway

Being proactive and squeezing couple time into the small gaps in life is not easy, but it may surprise you how much more connection you can create with just a few minor adjustments to your schedule and

routines. It doesn't always have to be a three-hour date. Sometimes just a quick check-in conversation can reorient your relationship in a more positive direction, and it may only take ten or fifteen minutes! For Heather and me (Peter), we had to get creative when we had three children in three years and had to look twice for ways to use our time productively. Putting the kids to bed early, turning off the television, and having a conversation was sometimes the closest thing we could find to quality time. But even those brief moments helped us reconnect as a couple. Hopefully, this date will show you how to find time together, even in the midst of errands!

Night at the Museum
Great Date

Heather and I (Peter) have lived in several cities over the course of our marriage. We started in Los Angeles, moved to Missouri, and then Minneapolis, and now we live in Denver. In some ways, they are all very different places, but they do have an abundance of great museums and art galleries. Over our two decades of marriage, we have had the opportunity to visit many amazing museums. We've found that with a little research, it is not difficult to find promotional discounts or free admission days for most museums. Some museums and galleries have free admission with a suggested donation. On this date, you'll choose a local museum or gallery you and your sweetie can check out together.

The Idea

There are numerous museums and art galleries in every large city across the country. Perhaps you live within driving distance of the Getty Museum in Los Angeles, the Smithsonian in Washington, D.C., or the Guggenheim in New York City. What a gift to have access to some of the world's best collections. Some of these institutions house timeless art masterpieces, while others hold historical artifacts or scientific innovations. Some museums, such as the

International UFO Museum in Roswell, New Mexico, are just plain quirky. Even these strange collections can be fun in their own way. The important thing is that you're getting out on a date together!

Before Your Date

- Get online and search for museums and gallery options in your area.

- Check their websites and the local listings for discounts and free admission days.

- Discuss your options and make a plan that sounds like fun for both of you. Don't worry if you live a thousand miles from the Smithsonian. Even small museums such as the Louisville Slugger Bat Museum (in Kentucky) or the U.S. Hockey Hall of Fame (in northern Minnesota) can turn into a great date!

On Your Date

- Wear comfortable shoes. Some museum collections are huge and involve a lot of walking.

- Consider following a tour guide or taking advantage of a self-guided audio tour. Knowing the backstories for certain pieces can really increase the intrigue of your experience.

- Some museums are very particular about not touching anything, while others offer interactive experiences. Make sure you are clear about which type of exhibit you're visiting.

Talking Points

- What was the most interesting piece or artifact you saw recently?

- What made it so interesting to you? Was it the artist, the story, the era, the purpose, or something else?

- If you could attend any exhibit in the world, what do you wish you could see up close and personal?
- What is the best museum you've ever visited?
- In your opinion, what makes something a masterpiece?

Great Date Takeaway

One of the best things about walking through a museum or gallery can be taking the time to learn the stories behind the pieces and the inspiration that motivated the artists or inventors from different eras and cultures. Perhaps you noticed the process of trial and error many artists have gone through as their work evolved over time. Monet made many sketches, planning out his paintings before he completed something as exquisite as his *Water Lilies*. Henry Ford produced several cars before he came out with his Model T. A masterpiece doesn't just happen—it takes time, effort, and the perseverance to learn from attempts that come up short.

Your marriage is no different. You are slowly creating a legacy as the story of your relationship unfolds. Part of the story will be learning, growing, and overcoming the inevitable obstacles. Remember, your relationship can become a masterpiece you co-create over time.

At-Home
GREAT DATES

Time Travel
Great Date

If you are like most couples, your early days of dating included going to the movies. It is such an easy date choice, and who doesn't love a little entertainment! On this date, you'll have a chance to watch a movie from the first year you started dating and revisit those early feelings of falling in love.

The Idea

When Heather and I (Peter) started dating, we took pride in the fact that we didn't see a movie right away. But after the first couple of months of dating, we eventually broke down and went to several movies. The top five movies of 1993 included thrillers, suspense, and romantic comedy: *The Fugitive*, *The Firm*, *Jurassic Park*, *Mrs. Doubtfire*, and *Sleepless in Seattle*. Just like a song or a favorite restaurant can be associated with this phase of your relationship, a movie you saw together in your early dating days can reconnect you with that very special time. Unless you're a brand-new couple, the movies you saw will no longer be in theaters, so you can save money by renting it or streaming it online.

Before Your Date

- Think back to the year you started dating each other. A quick web search can reveal the top movies from that year.

- Do you remember the first movie you saw together? That could be a great movie to watch again. Or perhaps there's a movie from that time you wished you had seen but never did. If you're like Heather and me, we really didn't like the first movie we saw together, but we would enjoy watching other options from 1993. Be flexible and have fun with this.

- If relevant, make sure the kids are entertained elsewhere so you can enjoy your movie and discussion uninterrupted.

On Your Date

- Consider a genre you both enjoy. Not everyone enjoys a horror flick, and likewise, not everyone wants to sit through a sappy romance. Try to find some middle ground you'll both find entertaining.

- Pop some popcorn and have fun traveling back in time and reconnecting with those early days of falling in love.

- Hold hands and/or snuggle up close to each other as you watch the movie!

- If you're not movie people, maybe you had a favorite song or television show from that era. Reconnect to your early days of dating by getting one of these other options.

- Once you've watched your movie, take some time to discuss the talking points below.

Talking Points

- If you just re-watched a movie from your early days of dating, how did the movie compare to your memories?

- What do you remember about asking (or being asked out) for your first date?

- What did you do together on your first date? Do you remember anything in particular from those early conversations?

- Did you have a defined "first date," or were you just hanging out and getting to know each other? At what point did you know your relationship had crossed over into something special or exclusive?

- In the beginning, what attracted you to each other?

- How often did you date in those early days—once a week? several times a week? How does that compare to your dating frequency now?

Great Date Takeaway

Movies are fun, but falling in love is better! As a relationship progresses from attraction to infatuation, and eventually to a mature love, most couples are excited about dating and making time for each other. This movie date is designed to give you a fun and easy way to tap back into the excitement of falling in love. Reminiscing about romance and reconnecting with those powerful feelings can give your relationship a great boost. Remember to make dating a priority, like you did in the early days.

Beating the Blahs
Great Date

The Idea

Are the blahs getting you down? Is the weather too hot or too cold? Are your finances "under water"? Is your to-do list endless, and you're just too tired to plan a date? We know the feeling. We've been there. Don't despair. It might just be a great time for a Beating the Blahs Date.

Before Your Date

Decide on your own approach to this date. We have two suggestions:

1. *Get out of your own comfort zone by doing something out of character.* Brainstorm what that might include, or consider the following suggestions:

    Have a picnic on the living room floor. Cushions, a checkered tablecloth, cold cuts, cheeses, and French bread could be a fun simple dinner and a good way to beat boredom.

    If you have a fireplace, roast hot dogs or make s'mores.

    Pull out your umbrella and take a walk in the rain.

Try a new recipe you haven't tried before.

Dust off and enjoy some board games you haven't played for years.

2. *Focus your date on chasing away someone else's blahs.* You might choose from the following or come up with your own ways to be an encourager:

Make a list of friends you haven't contacted in a long time, and on your date write or call several friends just to say hello.

Plan to visit a nursing home or hospital to cheer up a friend or relative.

Bake cookies and take them to someone you know who is going through a hard time.

On Your Date

- Don't talk about problems or issues that are weighing you down. If something comes up, table it for another time.
- Enjoy kicking back and just enjoying each other's company.

Talking Points

- Who do you know who is going through a hard time? Could you reach out and encourage them?
- How does it feel to do something out of character?
- What could be on your go-to list the next time you get the blahs?
- What can you celebrate that is going well instead of focusing on the blahs?

Great Date Takeaway

It's so easy to focus on the negative, and before we know it we are discouraged and have a bad case of the blahs. When we go down that negative path, there is only one thing to do: make a U-turn. *Quickly.* Let this date encourage you to concentrate on the positives and to appreciate each other. Then choose to give daily affirmations. Before long, you'll be tracking together down a pleasant path. The blahs will be history—at least for now.

Game Night
Great Date

Want to have more fun in your marriage? Try playing some games together! Playing a game with your spouse is a great way to have an inexpensive date no matter what the weather. This date can be a stay-at-home date, or you can take your game to a favorite coffee shop, restaurant, or even a park.

The Idea

Game night. It's a good excuse to turn off the screens, relax, and just play while you connect as a couple. Choose a game that is easily played with two people. There are games that rely more on luck and others that depend on skill. Depending on how competitive you and your spouse can be with each other, you may want to choose a game that will lead to less competition and more fun and laughter.

Peter and I (Heather) didn't have a TV for our first year of marriage. This gave us plenty of time to play different games together. We found some games required strategy, such as Mancala or Yahtzee, while others, such as Scrabble, required a lot more thinking and concentration. Still more games, like Uno, were a lot more about the luck of the draw or roll of the dice. These games

were usually relaxing and gave us an opportunity to talk about the day and discuss other topics while we played.

You may consider having a regular game night. Every evening, my parents play a game of Tri-Ominos. It gives them a chance to unwind, talk, and keep their minds sharp. They enjoy keeping track of their scores each night. The rule for them is that the loser has to put the game pieces away that evening.

Before Your Date

- Be aware of your game style (and personality) and choose games that will be more about fun and less about competition.
- You may want several games lined up to play, so if you finish one, you can keep going.
- Decide where you want to play your games—at home or out on the town.
- Be sure you have all the components needed to play the game or games you choose.
- If you like competition, create a prize, such as a back rub, for the winner.

On Your Date

- Have fun and enjoy your game! Be a good sport, win or lose.
- If time permits, play several rounds or several different games.

Talking Points

- When was the last time you played a game with your spouse?
- What kinds of games do you prefer—luck or strategy?

- What were your favorite childhood games?
- Which of you is more competitive? Did you notice this while playing games on your date?

Great Date Takeaway

When playing games, someone will win and someone will lose. Unfortunately, some couples have discussions or disagreements based on a similar outcome: a winner and a loser. This doesn't work well in a marriage. If one person feels defeated, the marriage takes a hit. Think about what it would be like if you adopted a "no losers" policy. What would be different if the next time you had a disagreement, you decided to change your goal from winning or getting your way to finding a solution you both can feel good about? Choose a mindset that makes your marriage the winner.

Coupon
Great Date

Sometimes we (the Arps) are procrastinators. We talk about all those fun things we never seem to get around to doing. Living in the metro Washington, D.C., area, our list could go on and on with things to experience, but we still procrastinate. A Coupon Great Date just may help move us (and you) closer to actually putting some feet on those potential great date ideas.

The Idea

On this date, you will brainstorm future fun dates together. You might think of this date as a "delayed gratification" date as you explore great dates for the future. Researching money-saving coupons will help keep future dates economical, so get ready for a fun evening.

Before Your Date

- Choose a time when you won't be interrupted for a couple of hours. This is a fun at-home date, or you may want to go out for coffee.
- Be sure to have pen and paper handy.

- Supplies needed to make your coupons are index cards, a paper punch, colored markers, and yarn or ribbon.

  Note: Why not just make coupons on your computer? You can, but sometimes it's just more fun to make them the old-fashioned way.

- It's great if you have access to the Internet on your smartphone or tablet.

On Your Date

- Brainstorm fun date ideas.
- You can draw from our $10 Great Dates or come up with others, such as flying kites together, watching the sun rise or set, playing miniature golf, or biking. Fill in with your own ideas:

  _____

  _____

  _____

  _____

- Both of you choose several dates and make your own date coupons. On the index cards, write out one date idea for each coupon. Punch a hole in each card. Tie coupons together with the colored yarn or ribbon, and *voilà*! You have a coupon book for future dates!

- You will want to hang your coupon books in a conspicuous place, maybe in the kitchen so you (as well as your children) will see it often. Then actually use the coupons!

- If you have an Internet connection, do an online search for coupons and see what you can find. You may find some great deals for future dates. Be sure to check expiration dates and details in the fine print to be sure it is something you'll be able to use.

71

Talking Points

- What were some of your favorite dates before you were married?

- What were some of the most fun "free" dates you have had?

- What is the best manufacturer's coupon you have ever used?

- What is one date you have always wanted to do but never got around to doing?

- What impact do your dating habits have on your children, or on family or friends who may be taking notice?

Great Date Takeaway

Part of the fun of dating your spouse is the anticipation factor—looking forward to the fun things you are going to do together. Take time to enjoy the process of thinking about and planning your future dates. Remember the proverb "A glad heart makes a happy face"?[4] Be glad you are modeling togetherness for your children. One of the greatest fears children have today is that Mom and Dad are going to split. Seeing you go out on dates can assure them you truly love each other and that their family is secure.

Create in the Kitchen
Great Date

Often the hardest part of cooking is *not* cooking the same old things night after night. Try getting out of the rut by creating something new together in the kitchen. Make a date of it!

The Idea

Our first Create in the Kitchen Date happened by accident. I (Heather) inadvertently purchased a package of chicken tenders instead of chicken breasts. Wanting to use the tenders in a new way, we went online and found a recipe for chicken satay, something we had never made before. We found we had most of the ingredients at home, but still needed some things that we weren't even sure would be at the local store: fish sauce, Thai red curry paste, and lemongrass? This was going to be an adventure! We found the new ingredients, and each worked together to make the marinade and peanut dipping sauce. We added some of our own ideas by wrapping the chicken in lettuce. The new flavors were amazing!

Before Your Date

- Find a new recipe to create your meal. Dust off the old cookbook you got as a wedding gift or find a new recipe online.

- If you are feeling adventurous, challenge yourselves to make a dish with at least two ingredients you have not used before.

- Check to see what ingredients you may already have and make a grocery list for the rest.

- Find an inexpensive grocery store.

- If time is an issue, you may want to break up the date by finding the recipes and buying the groceries in advance of the actual date evening.

On Your Date

- Once you begin cooking, talk about how you can work together. Who will do what part of the cooking so you can both enjoy the process? Perhaps you will want to switch up your usual roles in the kitchen. If you typically do the cooking and your spouse does the dishes, try switching it up for the evening. Maybe you normally work solo in the kitchen. Try working together.

- Music always makes work in the kitchen more fun. Play some music that goes with the type of food you're preparing to get you in the mood for your meal.

- Make the meal special. Set the table using your best dishes, and light some candles. We had our meal on the deck while watching the sunset. I'm not sure which we enjoyed more, the view or the food!

Talking Points

- Was your recipe a success? Rate it on a scale of 1 (not so good) to 10 (amazing).

- What do you think is the best meal you've ever eaten together? What made it so special?

- Just like cooking up the same old menus, our relationships can get stuck in a rut. What's one new thing you would be willing to do to spice up your marriage?

Great Date Takeaway

Trying something new can be a little intimidating, but it can also be inspiring! I was nervous about trying a recipe with ingredients that I wasn't even sure we could find. I wondered if I would even know how to prepare or use the ingredients. Once we found the courage to try something new, we were so impressed with the results that we are now inspired to try more new things. Maybe you too will find that cooking together is a fun marriage adventure that gives you courage to have more new experiences together.

Wedding Video
Great Date

If you are like most couples, you had someone film your wedding ceremony and reception. The video recording is probably sitting on a shelf or in a drawer somewhere, but it is time to locate it and revisit your past. Heather and I once hosted a wedding video party, where five other couples joined us with their wedding videos. We all agreed to show about ten minutes of the video footage, and then spent the remaining time reminiscing and laughing about how young everyone looked. What do you remember about your wedding day?

The Idea

On this date, you'll have the chance to remember your big day by watching your wedding video and discussing the significance of that event. What do you remember about your wedding ceremony, including the vows, songs, readings, and message? These components of your wedding service were significant on that day, and they are still significant today. You might also have footage of the wedding party and other guests who attended the wedding and/or reception. Those people stood with you on the day of your celebration, and they can still be a source of encouragement and support to you.

Have fun as you remember how everything came together—and maybe even a couple of the little things that didn't go as planned.

Before Your Date

- Start by finding your wedding video. If it is not in a format you can watch, spend a few dollars to get it transferred to a DVD or digital file. If, like the Arps, you don't have a wedding video, pull out your wedding pictures.

- Consider grabbing a note pad so you can jot down a few things that stand out to you about your service.

- It's also fun to look at your photo album, guest book, or ceremony program. Try to locate these items, as they will help you travel back in time.

On Your Date

- If you've been married a long time, you might laugh at the hairstyles or fashion choices. Have fun with this, but also pay attention to the content and messages conveyed on your big day.

- If you want to take it to the next level, see if you can find your wedding dress or tuxedo. If you're feeling really brave, try them on!

- Some couples were not able to have much of a ceremony. If this is true for you, talk about what kind of service you would plan today if you had the chance. Use the talking points below to consider the elements you would include.

Talking Points

- What is your best memory from your wedding day?

- How about the service itself? What stands out to you as you watch your video? Funniest moment? Biggest surprise? Most significant moment?

- Talk about your marriage vows. How do these promises take on new meaning today?

- Consider the message, songs, and readings offered at your service. Why were they significant then? What encouragement can you find in them today?

- If you could go back in time, what would you tell yourself on your wedding day?

Great Date Takeaway

Weddings are full of significance. It is a day when people show up to support and celebrate the new couple. Vows are spoken, toasts are offered, gifts are given, songs are sung, and it often culminates with a feast and a dance. You may have put a tremendous amount of time and energy into planning your wedding day, or you may have had a very small informal exchange of vows. As great as weddings are, they only last for a day. What is truly significant is the marriage that was formed on that day—*when two became one*—and hopefully lasts for a lifetime. Marriage is the foundation for healthy families that in turn form healthy communities. On this date, we hope you celebrate your marriage again as you reflect on all the elements that made that day special.

The Great Outdoors
GREAT DATES

20

Take a Hike (Together)
Great Date

If you're looking for a date that is good for your relationship and your health, this is it. Some of us (like me, Dave) like to relax by doing something constructive—my personal favorite is splitting logs. Others (like Claudia) like to relax and de-stress by talking. This date meets both of our needs. It's amazing how easy it is to talk to each other when you're out in nature.

The Idea

Pack your backpack and take a hike. For a really great hike (and if you're in good condition), consider an all-day hike. We love to hike along the Potomac River, and each year try to do a seven-mile hike that takes us up and down a rugged path with scenery that is simply amazing. Definitely worth it! Wherever you hike, get ready for some good exercise and conversation.

Before Your Date

- Research hiking trails near you. Most hiking guides will give helpful details, such as distance, difficulty, and other unique

features of the hike. You can also find helpful information on the Internet.

- Plan your course, and if available, print out a map.
- Take plenty of water and a couple of apples for an afternoon snack. Energy bars and nuts are also great hiking snacks.
- Pack your camera or smartphone.
- Bring and use sunscreen and bug spray if needed.

On Your Date

- Stay on the path.
- If you accidentally get on a path that is too difficult to navigate, be willing to turn around. (Claudia knows how I hate to turn around and retrace my steps, but sometimes it's the only thing to do!)
- If you have trekking poles, use them as needed.
- On narrow paths, take turns leading.
- It can be fun to use a walking app. We highly recommend the Walkmeter app, which costs about $5 (which leaves 5 bucks for snacks). It shows us everything we need to track our walk: maps, graphs, statistics, speed, and terrain. It also helps us find our way back if we get off the path. It was rated the best health care and fitness application (Appy Awards). You can search the web for walking apps and find one that is just right for you.
- Take along a pen and a couple of index cards to make notes. Hiking is our best brainstorming time.

Talking Points

- What are some of your favorite ways to relax and de-stress?
- If you made a map of your marriage journey so far, what would it look like?

- What were some of your mountain highs or valley lows?
- When was a time you needed to make a U-turn?
- How open are you to exploring new paths together?
- Where would you like to hike in the future? What is your dream hike?

Great Date Takeaway

Taking the time to walk together encourages a new appreciation of nature and the wonderful world that God created. Looking back at your marriage, marvel at where you've come from in your relationship and look forward to where you are going in the future.

Light the Fire
Great Date

There is something romantic and fun about a fire. Feelings of peace and calm seem to envelop us sitting near a campfire or watching the crackling flames in a fireplace. Growing up, it was not uncommon for my family (Heather's) to go camping with good friends and enjoy long evenings sitting around a campfire. Now Peter and I often sit with our children by the fire pit in our backyard, telling stories and roasting marshmallows.

The Idea

This date will give you a chance to have fun by the fire. Whether you are snuggling near one, camping next to one, cooking over one, or simply watching one flicker, this Light the Fire Date can warm up your marriage!

Before Your Date

- Brainstorm ideas of where you can experience a fire together. Look online for camping areas or parks that have fire pits.
- Perhaps you can build a bonfire in your own yard (depending on where you live) or build a fire in your fireplace.

- Plan and pack the needed supplies to be comfortable. This may include paper, matches, wood, chairs, or a blanket.

- Pack a snack, marshmallows for roasting, or even meat and vegetables to roast over the fire on skewers. Remember to bring drinks and paper products.

- If you're having a hard time coming up with a setting where you can get near a fire outdoors, think outside the box. Perhaps there's a restaurant, mall, or even a coffee shop with a fireplace. You could also light some candles and enjoy a romantic conversation at home.

- Always check for fire advisories and weather conditions, and be aware of local fire regulations.

On Your Date

- Enjoy relaxing or snuggling near the fire and watching its rhythm and energy.

- Roast your treats or meal over the fire.

- Try to be very present with each other. Focus on the moment and let the worries of the day fade away.

Talking Points

- Was it hard to build your fire? Did you have the right materials and conditions?

- What is your favorite memory of being around a campfire?

- Fire can be associated with many things, including relaxation, romance, or refinement. Talk about all three of these aspects of fire and how they currently relate to your life and relationship.

  Relaxation: What are some things that help you feel calm and relaxed? Is there a certain place or setting where you feel most at peace?

Romance: What's on your romantic wish list? Describe your ideal romantic date.

Refinement: Talk about what you would like to have less of in your life. How could you be refined as an individual?

Great Date Takeaway

You have to have the right materials, conditions, and effort to create a great fire. If you forget your matches, or run into wet or windy conditions, it can be quite difficult. Creating romance in your relationship can also take some effort. It is true that sometimes romance just happens, but usually you have to make a plan and put some energy into it. Make a mental note of your partner's romantic wish list for another day. Now that you are warmed up by the fire, keep the heat going in your relationship.

Movie on Location
Great Date

Most of the time, watching a movie at home has some common elements— comfortable chairs or a couch, some snacks, maybe a blanket. But what if you changed up the location? Now that you can watch movies on a number of devices, you are no longer limited to watching your movie at home or in a theater!

The Idea

This date was inspired by one couple we (the Larsons) know from Minnesota, who take their computer and watch a movie sitting near a local lake. They bring a blanket, bug spray for the mosquitos, and their favorite snacks. Renting a movie for under $10 is not a problem. There are several options to choose from. Once you have your movie, consider the setting where you'd like to watch it. Think about the type of movie you chose. Would a dark forest make an exciting setting for your suspense or thriller film? Would the beach be a fitting setting for the romantic comedy? If you're living in the city, find an open area where the stars can be seen clearly. You can take your movie to the top of a parking ramp, where there is a great view, and make it a "drive-in movie" by watching it from your car.

Before Your Date

- Select a movie you can download to a computer or other device.
- You may want to bring headphones so you can both hear the movie well.
- Decide together on a location that fits your movie and will be comfortable for both of you.
- Pop your popcorn. Pack your drinks and other snacks.
- Bring blankets, chairs, and whatever else is needed to be comfortable.
- If you'll be outside, remember sweaters, bug spray, and/or sunscreen!

On Your Date

- Get settled with your chairs and snacks so you can watch and hear the movie comfortably.
- Snuggle with each other as you watch your movie.

Talking Points

- What is your favorite movie?
- How did getting out of your normal routine and making a change of location affect your date?
- How did the location of your date affect your thoughts or experience of the movie?
- What is another movie you would like to watch in a new location for another date?

Great Date Takeaway

Changing location can give you a new perspective on things. Watching your movie together in a new way will be remembered because you chose to try something different. It is true that we can be transformed by the renewing of our minds. Are there areas in your marriage that you could look at from a new perspective? Think about your roles as wife, husband, or parent. How would a new perspective about your role affect your marriage and family? Even a small change, like switching who drives the car or sleeping on the other side of the bed, can alter your perspective. Think about one area in which you would like to shake up your routine this week and see how even a small change can transform aspects of your marriage.

Little League
Great Date

We (the Larsons) love watching Little League baseball games. Our son, AJ, is at the age where he plays baseball in the spring and summer months. While the youth skills can range, and games are not always pretty, they are always fun and full of learning opportunities. This date will appeal to those who want to be outside, enjoy some fun competition, and do something low cost!

The Idea

Watch the weather forecast and pick a beautiful evening to head out to a local park or school athletic field to watch a youth sporting event. The particular sport is not important (soccer, football, baseball, whatever). Just look for a free or inexpensive sporting event that involves two teams, and then enjoy yourselves. Sit on your blanket or find a good seat in the stands and watch some (relatively) high-action sport! Pick a team and cheer for your club.

Before Your Date

- In the days leading up to your date, keep an eye out for busy parks or athletic fields, so you'll know where to find a game on your date.

- Check local websites or talk to your neighbors to find out about upcoming events.

- Plan on this date taking about two hours.

- If needed, use the Cheap Child Care Options (see section near the back of this book).

On Your Date

- If you have kids who are in sports, you can watch one of their games. Just make sure you have time as well to talk and interact privately as a couple. If you're the coach or team manager, this won't work! Find a spot to sit away from other parents you may know to facilitate your own conversation.

- Varsity sporting events may charge admission, but it will most likely be under $5 each. If you have not spent your $10 on admission, splurge on some refreshments.

- Take note to watch how the players, the coaches, and the parents interact.

Talking Points

- Try to find an example of good teamwork. How well do these kids support their fellow teammates? How do they handle mistakes and disappointments?

- Were you ever on a great team? What made it great?

- What type of coach appears to be more effective? Why?

- Are the parents and players respecting the rules and the referee or umpire?
- How is your relationship similar to a team? Who's your coach?

Great Date Takeaway

Whether you realize it or not, the two of you are a team. Every interaction (negative or positive) affects your team. You can either win together or lose together, but any notion of a win/lose is just a myth—you're on the same team! Just like the teammates you're watching, there is never a time where one player on the team wins while another player on the same team loses! Notice that teams and teammates are not perfect. The apostle Paul challenges us to make allowances for each other's faults and forgive anyone who offends us.[5] Great teams work together, try to stay positive (even when mistakes happen), respect the rules, and turn to their coach for guidance. We hope you can walk away from this date remembering that you're on the same team, and the same attributes of a successful team can apply to your relationship as well.

Find Our Pace
Great Date

Do you sometimes feel like your marriage is plodding along on autopilot? Lacking in momentum or excitement? Other times, you might feel like things are whirling a million miles an hour with the scenery whizzing by in a blur. Either way, here is an opportunity to talk about adjusting or changing your pace together as a couple.

The Idea

If you are always saying "slow down" or "catch up," then this date is for you. Whether you're a walker, jogger, or runner, you can have fun learning to pace each other and find your "couple pace." The idea is to find a trail or path that is good for walking and jogging. Intentionally walk or run together and see how good you are at adjusting your pace to each other.

Before Your Date

- Research the area for trails or places where you can go for a walk, jog, or run. You might want to search the web for local maps of parks and neighborhoods.

- Choose a location with a great trail, if possible, or map a path through a neighborhood that you have not explored before.
- Be flexible. You may want to have this date in the morning instead of the evening.
- Plan to wear comfortable clothes and shoes. Bring water along.

On Your Date

- Take a walk or run and experiment with a new pace.
- If one of you is typically a slow walker, try running or jogging together for a short distance. Notice how your body feels as you get your heart rate up and push yourself out of your comfort zone. Afterward, you may feel worn out but exhilarated once you've recovered. You may just feel out of breath and grateful you're not a runner.
- Walk some more and then try another short-distance run or jog. Is it easier or harder?
- If you are a runner, try slowing down to the other's walking pace. Take time to look around and take in your surroundings. Notice the trees and the flowers or the water.
- What is it like for you to slow down? Are you tempted to try to speed back up to your usual pace?

Talking Points

- How difficult was it to walk or run at the other's natural pace?
- If you're more the walker, how did it feel to jog together?
- If you are the more natural runner, how did it feel to slow down and smell the roses?
- What is your current pace in life? Are you walking, jogging, or racing through your days? Are you both on the same course?

- Talk about ways that you might deliberately change the pace of your life. If you need to slow down, how can you create more margin in your life? If you need to speed up, what are some ways you can add more excitement to your routine?

Great Date Takeaway

Just like learning to pace each other on this date, we need to learn to pace ourselves in life so we will have a margin for what's most important. If others looked at your life and your marriage, what would they say is most important to you? What difference would it make in our lives if we stopped and considered this truth? Would we be more committed to running with perseverance the race set before us? What might we need to throw off that is hindering and entangling us?[6] What are some things you could let go of so you have the time and resources to invest in and build a strong and enduring marriage?

Playground
Great Date

When the kids were little, Peter and I (Heather) would often take the family to a nearby park and let the kids swing and climb on the playground equipment. If we weren't busy giving someone a push on the swing or catching another as they came down from the slide, we found we had time to talk with each other. Now that the kids are older, it's time to have our own date at the playground.

The Idea

On this date, go to a playground and enjoy playing like children. Yes, actually play together! A playground is a perfect setting to bring fresh air and laughter into your relationship and will give your marriage a lift too.

Before Your Date

- Find a park near your home where there are swings, slides, and climbing equipment. A seesaw is a bonus!
- Choose a playground that isn't too busy with other families so you have an opportunity to really play together.

- Wear comfortable clothes and shoes for climbing, running, or whatever you might want to do.
- Plan to take bug spray, sunscreen, water, and snacks.
- Take a softball or Frisbee to add to the fun.

On Your Date

- Bring along a playful attitude (don't just sit on the park bench). Check out the playground equipment.
- Get out there and swing! "Get married" as you swing in sync together. Slide down the slides. Swing from the monkey bars and walk on the balance beams. Find your rhythm on a seesaw.
- Remember to drink water and stay hydrated. Playing like children can expend a lot of energy, but it's great exercise!
- It may feel awkward at first, but be willing to let go of the expectations of adult behavior and allow yourselves the opportunity to play like children.
- Take breaks and sit on the bench to enjoy conversation.

Talking Points

- What were your favorite playground games as a child?
- Laughter is good medicine. How can you encourage more laughter in your marriage and in your home?
- What activities do you most enjoy doing together as a couple?
- Think about the seesaw and the importance of balance and teamwork.
- A key part of life is learning how to play well with others. How willing are you to work together to help each other succeed and reach your goals?

Great Date Takeaway

Do you remember the proverb that says a joyful heart is good medicine, but a crushed spirit dries up the bones?[5] Taking time to laugh, play, and have fun together not only helps our physical health but also the health of our marriage. Dave and Claudia remind us, "Fun in marriage is serious business." Keep the fun and laughter going in your marriage. Commit to another great date doing an activity that you both enjoy!

26

Moonlight/Sunrise
Great Date

Are you a morning person? Invite your spouse on a Sunrise Stroll with you. Are you a night owl? Try a Moonlight Walk together.

The Idea

There is beauty all around us each day, but we often sleep right through it! When we (the Larsons) moved near the mountains, we found that the colors reflected on the mountains during a sunrise can be as beautiful or picturesque as the colors of the sunset. It's a great time to hear the birds singing and feel the cool night warming to day.

Peter and I have started having an after-dinner walk as the kids clean the kitchen. With the shorter days in autumn, our walks have become a Moonlight Walk. Walking in the moonlight gives us a chance to reflect on the positives in our lives, even as we walk in semidarkness.

Before Your Date

- Choose a time of day that will work well for both of your personalities. Don't drag the night owl out of bed too early

or it may not be fun for either of you. Likewise, don't keep the sleepy one up too late or you may find yourself dragging him or her home.

- Be willing to try a new time of day with a positive attitude. You can choose to make it an adventure no matter what may be your best time of day.

- If you choose a moonlight date, consider scheduling it for a full moon. In the winter months with shorter days, you may not have to wait as late to begin your Moonlight Walk.

- Brainstorm or search the web for a nearby destination where you can watch the beauty of the sunrise together or enjoy a moonlit walk. Consider locations where you can see the sun rise over a field, a body of water, woods, or a mountain.

- Pack a flashlight or two to light your path.

- Bring coffee to sip while you watch the break of day or moonlight reflection.

- Plan for adjustments in temperature as the sun comes up or the cool evening sets in. You may need to bring more layers or a blanket for snuggling.

- If your kids are old enough for you to slip out for a walk in the early evening, you can go for a Moonlight Walk without having to arrange for child care.

On Your Date

- Enjoy your walking date. Hold hands.

- Discuss the Talking Points listed below.

- Use all your senses to determine how different the day is before the sun rises and after it sets. Listen for new sounds. Look for new colors and the reflection of the light from the sun or moon. Smell the trees or the flowers. Feel the coolness of the air before the sun rises or after it sets.

Talking Points

- What is your favorite time of day? When are you the most and the least productive?

- As the world wakes up or goes to sleep, there are subtle sounds, smells, and sights that are often missed. What did you notice on your date that was interesting or unusual?

- If you could watch the sunset or sunrise together anywhere in the world, where would it be?

Great Date Takeaway

On this date, you experienced some of the beauty that is around you—beauty often missed because you are either sleeping or simply overlooking what is there to enjoy. We may drive by the same beautiful oak tree so many times that it just becomes part of the landscape. Walking during a sunrise or a sunset gives you the opportunity to wake up your senses to God's beauty in creation. Just as there is beauty in the oak tree or the delicate flower, each of us is fearfully and wonderfully made. Take time to notice the beauty your spouse brings to your life.

Marriage
Pick-Me-Up
GREAT DATES

Family Tree
Great Date

What do you know about your family history? Dave's grandparents eloped in a horse-drawn carriage and were married down by a river. His other grandmother owned the very first car in Gilmer County in the North Georgia mountains. Today, we have the green blanket she used to keep warm as she forged streams in her Model T. Claudia's family tree can be traced back to George Walker, who "walked" for the king of England (whatever that means). We have always enjoyed looking into our family tree, and on this date you can learn more about yours.

The Idea

Have a Family Tree Date and fill in some of the branches on your own family tree. Plan an evening to delve into your family history. Before or on your date you can interview older relatives. Check out family Bibles and records, or check out genealogy websites. On this date, you will begin to piece together your own family history.

Before Your Date

- Interview as many relatives as you can before your date. There is no better way to get stories and memories than from those who experienced them firsthand. Also, talk to the oldest members of your family first to see what they may remember. Often it takes several people remembering information to get the whole picture. Who knows what you'll discover!

- You might want to do some initial research on your family history before your date. There are a number of websites that tell you how to get started. Just search *genealogy* or try www.ancestry.com. Most sites initially offer free information. (This could also be part of your date night.)

- Buy a sheet of poster paper so you can draw your family tree. You could also do this on your computer. Be prepared to record what you discover about your ancestors.

On Your Date

- Together, continue to search the web and see what you can find about your family history.

- Call and talk to older relatives. Put your phone on speaker mode so you both can be in on the conversations.

- Using the poster paper, sketch out your family tree and fill in all the information you have.

Talking Points

- What new insights have you gained about your family? What surprised you?

- Are there events or things your relatives have done that need to be remembered and passed down for future generations? For instance, Dave's grandmother started a number of country churches in the county where she lived. There is even a

106

stained-glass window in the First Baptist Church commemorating her dedication.

- Did any of your relatives do anything historically significant or noteworthy? For instance, did any of your ancestors fight in the Civil War? Revolutionary War? World War I or II?

- Did you discover any skeletons in the closet you would like to leave there?

- What lessons have you learned from your family research that you find inspiring?

- How do you want your future family to remember you and your family?

Great Date Takeaway

By discovering your family history, you can pass on a priceless heritage to your children and grandchildren. What traits did you inherit from your parents and grandparents? As you contemplate your answers, consider what you would like to pass on to future generations. Claudia's father had the gift of giving, and his investments in others are still impacting lives today. What will we leave behind that will make a positive difference in the lives of others? That's something worth thinking about.

Drive-Through
Great Date

We're not promoting fast foods, but our Drive-Through Date has value far beyond the food. You can actually learn a new communication technique by observing the ordering process at fast-food restaurants. Since your budget is only $10, plan to place small orders at several drive-through windows. On this great date, you can learn a helpful tool, perform a small observational experiment, and purchase treats all at the same time. Now, that's a great combo deal!

The Idea

Head out to several local fast-food restaurants that have drive-through windows. The key for this date is to make sure you use the drive-through lanes. Why? There is a great metaphor for effective communication that takes place in the drive-through. Years ago, consumer research revealed that customers would understandably become quite frustrated when they drove away and discovered their fast-food order was wrong. The main problem seemed to be the poor sound quality offered by the small speaker/microphone boxes into which customers would shout their orders. Smart business operators began to train their employees to repeat back what they thought the customer ordered. This simple step of double-checking

the order drastically reduced errors and increased customer satisfaction. Technology has now taken this double-checking to even greater lengths. As you go out for your Drive-Through Date, you can explore this fundamental principle of effective communication.

Before Your Date

- Start by deciding which drive-through restaurants you'd both like to visit. In most areas, there are many options to choose from. You can do this date at any time of day as you buy a drink, purchase a snack, get a meal, or simply have an after-dinner treat.

- Most fast-food restaurants have an inexpensive value menu and some healthier options these days, so take your time and find something you're both willing to eat. If you can't find food options you both like, try a coffee shop with a drive-through window that serves coffee, tea, or smoothies.

On Your Date

- You'll be trying to stick to your $10 budget, so keep this in mind as you place your orders.

- Pay close attention to the ordering process as you go through the drive-through lane. You'll be asked to reflect on what you see and hear in the Talking Points.

- While the drive-through lane may be fast, don't rush your date. Park, eat, and leave yourself some time to discuss the points below.

Talking Points

- Did they get your order correct?

- Technology has changed things in the drive-through world. Still, what methods were used to double-check the accuracy of your order?

- Listening is key to effective communication. Who in your life is a great listener, and what makes them effective?

- Do you or your spouse regularly double-check the accuracy of what you are hearing before you respond to each other?

- Take turns being the customer "placing your order." The speaker will go first by completing the following sentence: "In my opinion, the best part of my week was . . ." The listener will repeat back what they heard without interrupting, judging, or reacting to the message.

- What did it feel like to be listened to like this? Was it more difficult for you to be the speaker or the listener?

Great Date Takeaway

Experts agree that communication is foundational for successful relationships. Study after study has identified communication as the key ingredient for feeling emotionally connected, effectively solving problems, and making important decisions together. In all of this, the listening aspect of communication is often overlooked. How well do you listen to each other? The small acts of slowing down, withholding judgment, and checking out what you think you're hearing can dramatically change the course of a conversation. The wisdom of being slow to speak and quick to listen is powerful. While it may sound simple, it is not always easy to do! It takes self-control and practice. Just remember the example of the drive-through. If the process works for them, it will work for you too!

Marriage Checkup
Great Date

No matter how long you've been married, every couple should have marriage checkups. Think about it. Smart people get annual physicals and dental checkups to keep their bodies healthy. Shouldn't smart couples do the same for the health of their marriage? Of course! And the good news is, checking up on your marriage can be much more fun than going to the doctor for your yearly physical or to the dentist to get your teeth cleaned and examined.

The Idea

Go to your favorite coffee shop or bistro, or anyplace where you can talk privately. You might even want to go to a church that remains open to the public for prayer and meditation. The purpose of this date is to check in with each other about how you are doing as a couple. The fact that you are planning this date is a positive thing, and it will be even more so as you celebrate what's going well in your relationship and identify areas you might want to address in the future.

Before Your Date

- Plan a time when you can spare a couple of hours alone to talk.

- Go prepared to discover great things about your relationship.

- Be willing to talk about areas that both of you might want to work on and improve.

- Go with the attitude that you are a team—a strong partnership. This date is not a test. No competition here. It's going to be a win/win date that will move your marriage forward.

On Your Date

- Sit across from each other where it's quiet so you can talk and focus on each other.

- Together, make a list of the great things you already have going for you in your marriage.

- In sharing with each other, keep the conversation positive by using "I . . ." statements and avoiding "You . . ." statements and "Why . . ." questions.

Talking Points

- Take turns talking about what delights you most about your spouse.

- What are some of the best things that have happened to you as a couple in the past twelve months?

- What is one challenge you faced and surmounted together this past year?

- What challenges are you facing at the present time? How can you work together to surmount them?

- What are one or two goals you would like to set for the next twelve months? One couple we know has a Marriage Checkup Date each year on their anniversary. They celebrate their successes from the previous year and choose two or three new goals for the coming year.

Great Date Takeaway

You may find that this yearly checkup is one you'll look forward to, and it'll keep your relationship healthy and growing. One key to a great marriage is being intentional in setting goals and seeking wisdom from above. Remember that God is the great physician and the ultimate doctor of the soul of your marriage.

Volunteer
Great Date

On this date, you'll have the chance to bless someone else as you volunteer your time and energy to lend a helping hand.

The Idea

Not many people wake up thinking about where they can volunteer or serve others. Beyond this, very few would consider a service project to be a date! But in serving others, there are hidden opportunities to bless others and be blessed yourself! We (the Larsons) have helped pack meals for the hungry, and in doing so were reminded of how fortunate we are.

Volunteering and serving others helps us look beyond our own concerns and issues and provides a new perspective on those things we tend to think are so difficult in our own lives. When you volunteer as a couple, you enter into something bigger than yourselves, something purposeful and meaningful. We've never met anyone who regretted helping others.

Before Your Date

- Think about what type of cause you would both find meaningful. Do you have a concern for children, the elderly, or those struggling with illness? What about local groups that are helping the poor with food shelves or housing?

- Check around for some volunteer opportunities. You may have to look online or call some schools or churches to find good options.

- Consider helping an elderly neighbor or a friend who was recently widowed. Do you know couples with young children who may need a surprise break? For whom could you prepare a meal, wash a car, or clean out a garage?

- Once you've identified your mission, call to confirm the need for volunteers during the time you're available. You may have to be flexible with your schedule.

- Make sure you pick something you can actually do and do together. Look for something that lends itself to your natural gifts. If you love to cook or meet new people, serving at a shelter may be a perfect fit. If you'd rather do something quietly together, you could rake an elderly neighbor's yard or tend their garden.

On Your Date

- Work side by side and encourage one another as much as possible.

- Dive in 100 percent for the time you're serving. Try to leave your personal concerns behind and focus on helping others.

Talking Points

- How did serving others change your perspective on your own problems or stressors?

- Everyone has gifts and abilities. Tell your spouse one thing you observed in them that is a gift that blesses others.

- How do you serve one another in your relationship? Discuss a specific instance where you have noticed your spouse serving you.

- What are you thankful for today?

Great Date Takeaway

It is easy to get wrapped up in our own thoughts, feelings, and concerns, and become self-absorbed or lose proper perspective on life. Serving others as a couple helps us to be thankful for the many blessings in our lives. It is an expression of love that allows us to exercise our gifts and abilities. It also helps us to stop taking things for granted. In fact, it can be so beneficial to help others in need that psychologists have been known to prescribe it for those suffering from depression. We hope your simple act of service can be a boost to you, your relationship, and those you've helped!

Bucket List
Great Date

Woulda. Coulda. Shoulda. What's on your list? It may not be too late to turn some of what you would like to do into reality. That's what the Bucket List Date is all about. This last year Claudia and I (Dave) had our own Bucket List Date and made a list of things we would like to do. For instance, two items on our list are hiking Old Rag (one of the most challenging hikes in the Shenandoah National Park) and reconnecting with old friends we haven't seen for years. We just fulfilled one of them! Recently, we reconnected with old army friends we knew in Germany more than forty years ago. What fun it was to catch up after all these years. We had a great double date together as we reminisced about our army days. Still to do is hiking Old Rag.

The Idea

On this date you can dream about the experiences you would like to have together, such as places you would like to visit, old friends you would like to reconnect with, challenges you would like to surmount together, and so on. On your date, you can make your own bucket list and talk about how to begin to check off your list.

Before Your Date

- Decide on the location for this date. If the weather permits, this would be a fun date to have outside—maybe on a hike or at a park. It could also be a fun at-home date. We can picture this as a great date sitting on the floor by a roaring fire with cups of hot chocolate.

- Spend some time priming the pump, thinking about the future and what you might like to do together. What projects might you tackle? What course or class could you take together? What sport or skill would you like to learn?

- You could pull out travel books or research websites, highlighting places you would like to visit someday. Or you could take your notebook along with you on your date and explore together.

On Your Date

- Brainstorm together and make a bucket list of what you both want to do as a couple while you still can.

- Prioritize your list and talk about what might actually be possible.

- Choose one, two, or three items from your list to begin pursuing.

Talking Points

- Share with each other how you would finish the following statements:

  If money were no object, I would like to . . .
  My most favorite place in the whole world is . . .
  The place I would most like to visit (or revisit) is . . .
  One thing I would like to learn is . . .

Great Date Takeaway

Dreaming together is not only fun, it's the beginning of fulfilling your dreams. Choosing a goal to work toward can foster fun and excitement and overcome boredom in your relationship. Marriage is a journey, not a destination. You should always have room for dreams, and a bucket list helps with accomplishing them along the way.

Gratitude
Great Date

Many people work in generally thankless jobs, including teachers, health-care professionals, postal workers, and those who diligently haul away waste and recyclable materials. These individuals, working to serve others, could use a note or gesture of appreciation. Think about people who have a positive influence in your life— perhaps a pastor, friend, or mentor you could thank and serve in some way. A Gratitude Date gives you the opportunity to identify helpful people in your life and express your appreciation to them.

The Idea

When our three children were young, it was difficult for Peter and I (Heather) to find the time to volunteer and help others the way we typically enjoy doing. Since we didn't have more time to give, we wanted to thank those who were volunteering with our kids at church or school. Often those working with our kids were young adults who appreciated a family dinner. We would ask the kids to invite their volunteer leaders for a family meal.

My favorite story was when our youngest went to a day camp and wanted to ask the two volunteers "who were friends with each other" for dinner. I was confused by this description, but I smiled

when I found she wanted to ask a couple who had been married for over twenty-five years to join us for dinner. After hosting this couple for a thank-you dinner, they became a special part of our family for years to come.

Besides hosting someone for dinner, there are many ways you can show some appreciation to the people who volunteer or serve in your life. Perhaps there is someone who would feel loved by a handwritten note. You may even want to include a $5 gift card.

Before Your Date

- List the people you appreciate in your life. Decide together whom you want to thank in some way. If your budget and time allows, you may choose more than one person.

- Brainstorm creative and meaningful ways to show your appreciation together, such as doing yard work, house cleaning, laundry, delivering a meal, free babysitting, writing thank-you notes, making cookies for a friend, or inviting someone for a cup of coffee.

- Once you've got your plan in mind, set a time for your date. It may take some courage to step out and thank someone. If you prefer, you can find a way to thank them anonymously.

- Plan to take what you need to accomplish your task. If you're cleaning for someone, bring your own cleaning supplies. If raking someone's yard, don't forget the bags.

On Your Date

- Follow through with your thank-you plan.

- You may want to extend your date by treating yourselves to a coffee or treat.

- Thank yourselves for taking time to thank others!

Talking Points

- How did it feel to work together to thank someone else?
- What was the most difficult thing about serving or thanking others in this way?
- How did taking the time and energy to thank someone affect you individually? As a couple? Those you served?
- How can you make thanking others a more frequent habit in your marriage?
- What is one meaningful way you can thank your spouse?

Great Date Takeaway

You have heard it said, it is more blessed to give than to receive.[6] Now you have experienced the encouragement that comes from taking the time to thank someone in a meaningful way. Looking for ways to show appreciation and gratitude will change your perspective. What are the ways your spouse would appreciate being shown gratitude? How would showing or saying "thank you" for the little things your spouse does each day affect your relationship? Choose an attitude of gratitude!

Romantic
GREAT DATES

33

Dining Under the Stars
Great Date

If you've been dreaming of a romantic formal dinner for two but your budget says "No way!"—keep reading. We have a great date for you. While "formal" usually means expensive, we'll show you a way to create your own five-star dining experience on a budget and make your spouse the star of the evening.

The Idea

Formal dinners aren't only reserved for expensive restaurants. You can experience your own elegant dinner with all the trimmings right out under the stars. And by packing your own dinner, you'll save big bucks. Choose a local park that lends itself to romance. Check the weather forecast and choose an evening when the stars should be out. Invite your spouse to a unique dining experience and volunteer to pick up the tab. You might want to keep the location and details a secret. Get ready for an evening out. But first, you've got to read this email from Jeanne Barsby, who pulled off an amazing anniversary celebration without breaking the bank. While she spent more than $10, you could improvise and pull this date off within the $10 limit. Plus, who says you can't splurge once in a while?

Dear David and Claudia,

Friday was our 10th anniversary. We have six kids between us, and the thought of doing anything was stressing out my husband because of the cost involved. So I followed your suggestion to have our own five-star dinner in a park near our home. I was excited about this idea and decided to surprise my husband. I picked a spot at one of our parks that had a lake, and told my husband I had found a five-star restaurant at a great deal and made reservations for us at 8 pm. Since we have six kids ranging from 20 years to 19 months, and I had a brother to help, they all got excited and were totally on board.

I rented a tablecloth and chair covers for the table and chairs. I then used my best china, and went to a secondhand store for the candlestick holders, linen napkins, and two vases for the single red roses. I set everything up at home the way I wanted the table to look and showed my oldest, and then took pictures. Then I bought white dress shirts (secondhand) for all the kids and had them wear black pants. I made a "to-go" order at a restaurant around the corner so they could just pick it up. Then I loaded up the car and sent them to the park at 6:30 pm with all the fixings to set it up.

My husband was confused when we pulled into a park instead of a restaurant, and even more confused when we got out of the car. Then he saw the table setting on the shore! He was so surprised . . . then asked if I'd had it catered. I said, "Yes, but don't worry, I got a great deal!" Then our 10- and 8-year-olds walked down with our salad bowls. He was overjoyed, and actually teared up. Then our 14-year-old and 19-month-old brought more dishes for the meal (it was so cute watching him walking down the hill in his little white and black outfit). For every course they walked down in pairs.

It was a magical night and one both of us will never forget! Thank you so much for this suggestion! We had our five-star restaurant date for our anniversary, our kids got to be a part of it, and my husband didn't have to worry about the cost. The

grand total was $52 for everything. Thanks for reminding me that it is not always about what someone else provides. We have the power to create our own experiences. God bless you!

Before Your Date

- Research romantic parks and locations near you. Find a park with a picnic table and benches—or you could take your own folding table and chairs.

- Invite your spouse for a unique dining experience, keeping the location and details to yourself.

- Plan your dinner menu. Look in your freezer and pantry and see what you can find.

- Recruit help—your children, friends, relatives?

- Take along a tablecloth, napkins, china, or whatever you have to make it "formal." A long-stemmed red rose, bud vase, candleholder with candles, and/or tea light candles will create a romantic atmosphere and add a five-star touch to the evening. If it's spring or summer, a vase of wild flowers could be equally romantic.

- Take along a flashlight or two.

- Take your favorite music. Download favorite romantic songs you have enjoyed together.

- Take your camera or smartphone to capture the moment in pictures.

- Wear a favorite dress, suit, or sports coat. Take along a sweater or scarf in case the evening turns cool.

On Your Date

- Let your children (or friends) be your waiters and serve the dinner.

- Enjoy romantic music and take pictures during the dinner.

Talking Points

- Are there some favorite times together that you would rate five-star?
- What romantic times together do you both remember?
- What makes an evening or outing truly romantic for you?

Great Date Takeaway

Great moments don't have to cost an arm and a leg, and as Jeanne can attest, you can take the initiative and make it happen. We (the Arps) have been married over fifty years, and looking back, our most romantic times had very little to do with spending a lot of money. They were the result of thoughtfulness and choosing to encourage and surprise the other. How can you create a little romance this week?

At-Home Spa
Great Date

A date for two at a spa sounds delightful but expensive, and definitely over a $10 budget. Why not create a spa right in your own home? With a little imagination, you just might be able to pull off a relaxing and romantic spa date for two.

The Idea

Enjoy an At-Home Spa Date by creating a romantic atmosphere with things you already have in your home. Top it off with body massages, heated towels, and chocolate-covered strawberries! This is sure to be a date to remember!

> *Note:* This is a good date for one spouse to plan for the other as a surprise.

Before Your Date

- Make arrangements for the children to be out of the home for the evening with a relative or friend.
- Look through your home for accessories that would add to the spa feeling, such as scented candles, bath salts, bubble bath

(you could substitute children's shampoo), or scented oil (even baby oil will work). Add flowers or a houseplant. Use candles and turn the lights down low. Choose your favorite romantic and relaxing music for the evening.

- Pull out those nice towels you've been saving for guests. When ready to use them on your date, you can warm them in the dryer for a luxurious touch.

- Before your date, stage your home. Prepare the bathroom for a soaking bath. If you have a fireplace, place a blanket on the floor in front of a roaring fire for a great massage.

- Put together a light meal of finger foods and drinks. For a romantic dessert you can prepare ahead of time, try strawberries or other fruit dipped in chocolate. Here's a simple recipe.

Chocolate-Covered Strawberries

Ingredients (well within your $10 budget):
  Strawberries (washed and dried well—chocolate will not stick to damp fruit)
  1 package of chocolate chips
  1 teaspoon oil

Directions:
  Melt the chocolate chips in a double boiler. Add a small amount of oil. When the chocolate is melted, dip the strawberries into the chocolate. Place the chocolate-covered strawberries on parchment paper and put in the refrigerator for several hours.

- Ask your spouse what time he or she expects to arrive home, then have the stage set for his/her arrival (candles lit and music playing, lights turned down low). Think romance.

On Your Date

- When your spouse arrives home, greet him or her with a hug and kiss and invitation to enjoy an At-Home Spa Date. Let him or her relax while you run a hot bubble bath and light candles around the tub.

- While your spouse soaks and relaxes, set out finger foods and drinks on the blanket in front of the fireplace in the candlelit room. (The fire is optional—romance is not.)

- Heat a fresh towel in the dryer and invite him or her to join you on the blanket by the fire.

- Offer to give a comforting, soothing body massage.

- Serve the chocolate-covered strawberries and enjoy the rest of the evening!

Talking Points

- How did it feel to be the giver or the receiver of this At-Home Spa Date?

- What are the best stress relievers for you? What helps you relax and unwind?

- Did you have a favorite part of this date?

- What did you think of the strawberries?

Great Date Takeaway

Most people would agree that it is more blessed to give than to receive. Yet so many times we focus on what we want from others and not what we can give. In an enriched, healthy marriage, partners need to focus on being other-centered. As you go through the coming week, you might want to look for gifts of love you can give to your spouse. You may find that you are the one who is most blessed.

Let's Rumba
Great Date

If you haven't been dancing in a while, maybe a long while, now is a good time to venture out but with a different twist (no pun intended). Try dancing at home! If dancing is outside your comfort zone, all the better. Sometimes we need to do something new to add a little adventure to our marriage, so try a dancing date.

The Idea

On this date you'll learn some new dance steps, plus more about the way you are able to work together as a team. Some dance styles have more structure than others, where one person leads and the other follows. Think of the popular show *Dancing With the Stars*. The challenge is to learn how to flow together and complement each other. The art of dancing may just teach you a lot about the art of marriage.

Before Your Date

- Begin by making a list of dances you already know and start with those. The old and familiar will be good practice as a warm-up before learning some new steps.

- Some dances to consider: hip-hop, waltz, two-step, tango, cha-cha, country line dancing. You get the idea.

- Do a web search for *free dance lessons*. You will find these online, complete with instructions, music, and so on.

- Plan on spending one to two hours on this date, giving yourselves time for a great discussion after you've worn yourselves out on the dance floor.

On Your Date

- Roll up the rug and start with a dance that you already know and feel comfortable with.

- For the partner who is a little reluctant, give it your best shot. Consider it a gift of love.

- Cooperate with your partner and see what you can learn from this experience. Who is the natural leader?

Talking Points

- Which style or styles of dancing do you prefer?

- What did you find most stressful about dancing? What was most enjoyable?

- Did you learn something new about each other?

- Would you like to have this date again? Try some different styles of dance?

Great Date Takeaway

There is more to this date than learning a new dance step. While it is fun and part of the adventure, possibly the biggest takeaway is what you learn about each other and how you can better work together as a team. Remember: Two are better than one.[7]

133

Three Wishes
Great Date

The Idea

How many times do we use the phrase *I wish*? Here's a date idea in which some of your spouse's romantic wishes just might come true. As silly as this may sound, we have a friend who met her husband one evening at the door wearing a tutu, complete with wings. "Tonight, I'm your fairy godmother," she announced, "and I will grant you three wishes." The evening progressed from there.

Before Your Date

- This date works best as a surprise date. Choose your timing wisely.

- You might not want to dress as a fairy godmother, but you could choose an alluring outfit you know your spouse likes.

- If you have children, make arrangements for their care on this evening—a good time for grandparents to step in. (If your parents don't live close by, consider the Cheap Child Care Options near the back of this book.)

- Serve simple finger foods and dessert for the evening.

- Set a romantic atmosphere by turning the lights low and setting out candles.

- Choose your spouse's favorite playlist of romance tunes and get ready for a great evening.

On Your Date

- Welcome your spouse at the door, explaining that you will grant him (or her) three wishes.

- *Caution:* Some might find agreeing to three unqualified wishes a bit uncomfortable and threatening. What if your partner asks you to do something you don't want to do? If you have concerns, instead ask for five wishes, and then choose the three that you're most comfortable granting. You could also have a prepared list of wishes to choose from, such as a back rub with hot oil, a foot massage, a shower for two, and so on. (This is also helpful if your partner is so completely surprised that he or she can't think!)

- Relax together and enjoy bringing pleasure to the one with whom you have chosen to share your life.

Talking Points

- What have been some of your most romantic moments?

- What are some good elements of a romantic evening?

- Describe what it feels like to be the giver in this setting or what it feels like to be the receiver.

- In your busy lives, what generally gets in the way of romance?

- How can you be more intentional in keeping romance alive in your marriage?

Great Date Takeaway

Keeping romance alive over the years requires a lot of give and take on the part of each of you. It requires being intentional and thoughtful toward the other person. This date helps to highlight the importance of both giving and receiving pleasure. Think about your experience. Was it fun being the giver? Was it fun being the receiver? Sometimes it may be harder to be the receiver than the giver. What about the element of surprise? Think of little ways you can surprise each other with spontaneous hugs or kisses, or a text or email message saying, "I love you" or "I'm thinking about you." Be intentional about creating romance, and both of you will enjoy the results.

37

Hotel Lobby
Great Date

Claudia and I (Dave) log a lot of time in hotels. Usually, we're there for a conference or seminar and not for a great date, but occasionally we have time to enjoy the ambience of the setting. Here's what we do. When we have a few minutes to chill and relax, we find a comfortable couch in the hotel lobby and just have fun watching people come and go. Once in Memphis, Tennessee, we also watched ducks! Yes, the Peabody actually has a duck pond in its lobby. It's amazing what you can discover in hotel lobbies.

The Idea

Go to an upscale hotel and enjoy the sights and sounds. It can be a refreshing change for the typical date night. Plus it's a date that doesn't break the bank—it's basically free. Enjoy watching people come and go in the hotel. One couple extended their Hotel Date by visiting several hotels on the same evening. They called it their Hotel Lobby Hopping Date. For the adventuresome, go separately and "accidently" meet up with each other. We know it sounds a bit corny, but it's actually fun to flirt and start up a conversation with each other. (How long has it been since you flirted with your spouse?)

Before Your Date

- Research hotels in your area. Online you'll find pictures, and they usually include pictures of the lobbies. You can choose the more romantic ones to visit.

- Before your date, spend some time thinking about your relationship history and the first time you met.

On Your Date

- Enjoy people-watching. Fantasize about their lives—where are they from, what might bring them to this hotel?

- If strangers were watching you, what might they observe? Would they assume you were married? Look at your spouse through the eyes of a stranger. What do you find intriguing?

- Enjoy reminiscing about the first time you met.

- If the hotel staff isn't too busy, and if it's vacant, they may be willing to show you the honeymoon suite. After all, you might want to reserve it for a tenth, twenty-fifth, or fiftieth anniversary! Yes, even after fifty years you can still be dating and celebrating your marriage.

- To extend this date, visit other hotel lobbies on the same evening.

Talking Points

- What do you like about this hotel? Would it be a good setting for an overnight getaway?

- Talk about the first time you saw each other. What attracted you to your spouse? What do you think attracted your spouse to you?

- What are some of your spouse's most endearing qualities?

Great Date Takeaway

Dating can enrich your marriage, but if you add the element of doing something new or a bit out of your norm, you may benefit even more. Also, revisiting your memories of when you first met and fell in love can rekindle romance and all kinds of other good things.

38

Surprise Me!
Great Date

Not everyone loves a surprise, but it can certainly be a fun way to spice things up in your relationship. On this date, you'll have a chance to plan a meaningful (and inexpensive) surprise for each other. Take time to flex your romantic and creative muscles.

The Idea

Each of you should plan your surprise for the other prior to your date. Consider including three basic elements as you make your plans: location, an object, and a significant message.

For example, I (Peter) might drive Heather to our family cabin (location), have her sit on the deck (object), and reminisce about how she helped build that deck twenty years ago when we were just starting to date (significant message). She might take me to Lake Harriet (location), buy us each an ice cream cone (object), and suggest that we take more walks together on nice summer evenings (significant message). One wife took her husband to the location of their first date and produced a movie ticket stub she had saved from that first evening together. She shared her memories of those early days of falling in love and how meaningful they were

to her. Once you reveal your surprise, talk through some of the discussion questions.

Before Your Date

- Make your plan. Take time to think through the location, object, and significant message you want to share. Your surprise can be about the past (memory), future (hope), or present (something of current significance).

- Remember, you don't have to spend a lot of money to have fun on this date.

- Depending on the distance of your location, decide if you'll both do surprise "reveals" on the same date or turn this date idea into two separate outings.

- If needed, arrange for child care.

On Your Date

- Trying to be creative is a challenge for some individuals. Don't be critical of how your sweetie did with this task. Some people will naturally be more creative or romantic than others.

- If you have to travel far to reveal your surprise, this date can become time consuming. In that case, turn it into two dates and take turns revealing your surprise.

- Be positive and have fun!

Talking Points

- Why do you think your spouse chose this location? (If you get the first part correct, try guessing what the object and significant message might be.)

- It's all right if you can't guess; that's part of the surprise. Begin by asking the following questions:

  "Why did you bring me to this location?"

  "What object have you chosen, and what does it represent?"

  "What significant memory, message, or future hope would you like to share with me?"

- Discuss your reactions to the surprise.

- What do you like most about the surprise your partner planned? How have you surprised each other on other occasions?

Great Date Takeaway

Sometimes the most powerful thing we can do for our spouse is to show them we're thinking about them and our relationship. This simple concept gives you a chance to reconnect with a great memory, place the spotlight on something that is currently going well, or express a positive wish for the future of your relationship. Throughout history, people have erected memorials, monuments, or statues to remember significant events, places, and people. These concepts relate to many areas of life—a successful business honors its past, pays attention to the current marketplace, and sets goals for the future. A successful relationship is no different. Great relationships don't just happen, so let this fun Surprise Me Date be a positive boost for the two of you this week!

Seasonal Specials
GREAT DATES

39

Spring Festival
Great Date

All around the country you can find spring festivals celebrating the end of winter and the beginning of spring. Spring festivals are a wonderful setting for a great spring date. We (the Arps) live in northern Virginia, and the Cherry Blossom Festival is our favorite. Over a century ago, as a gift from Japan, more than three thousand cherry trees were shipped to America. The first Cherry Blossom Festival was organized in 1935, and to this day the strikingly beautiful blooms represent spring for Washingtonians and tourists who come from far and near to enjoy their splendor. If you live near Washington, D.C., you can turn the Cherry Blossom Festival into a $10 Great Date, as many of the events are free.

The Idea

Attend a spring festival in your area. For years we lived in Knoxville, Tennessee, where the highlight of spring is the Dogwood Festival. Check in your area for spring festivals celebrating the arrival of spring. Many of the events (over several weeks) may be free, including the opening ceremonies, fireworks, and concerts.

145

Before Your Date

- Do your research. Find spring festivals near your community and choose one to attend.
- What days and time of the day are the best to avoid crowds? Where is the best parking?
- If there is an opening ceremony, look for free tickets online.
- If needed, plan to arrive early to find a free parking space.
- Wear comfortable clothing and shoes and be prepared to walk.
- Bring your camera or smartphone to capture pictures.
- Plan for traffic with extra snacks and water in your car for the ride home.

On Your Date

- Allow plenty of time, and pace yourself.
- Take lots of pictures.
- Take breaks and enjoy people-watching as well as all the sights and sounds of the festival.

Talking Points

- How much do you know about the history of the spring festival in your community?
- What do you like most about spring?
- Name your favorite blossoming trees and flowers.

Great Date Takeaway

We've all heard the adage "Stop and smell the roses." We could add, "Take time to smell and enjoy the cherry blossoms"—or dogwoods, spring flowers, fresh air, or whatever spring offers you in your part of the world. Life is too wonderful to hurry through it. Take time for your marriage today and enjoy the beauty of spring.

Green Thumb
Great Date

When spring arrives, do you look forward to getting outside and getting your hands dirty? If so, this date may be just right for you. If you're not a gardener, don't worry. Heather and I (Peter) don't have green thumbs, but we have fun experimenting with growing various vegetables and herbs that we can use in our kitchen. Now is the time to get ready for this simple springtime date as you picture the amazing garden you could have come summer.

The Idea

Springtime is when gardeners start to get excited, anticipating the flowers, herbs, fruits, and vegetables that will populate their garden all summer long. Choose some seeds and/or seedlings to plant together on this Green Thumb Date. Don't worry; you don't need a large garden. If you have space to plant your seeds outdoors, that's great. If not, you can plant them in an indoor pot and move them out to a deck or balcony when it gets warmer.

Before Your Date

- Decide what you want to plant and where you're going to plant your seeds and/or seedlings. This will determine if you're going to need a pot and some potting soil, or some compost and a hoe to turn over the dirt in an existing garden space.

- Plan on this date taking two to three hours. Make sure you allow not only for the shopping but also for the planting.

- Seeds and soil are inexpensive, so staying under your $10 budget should not be a problem. Friends or neighbors might be willing to share some of their perennials that are just poking their heads through the soil.

On Your Date

- Find a local nursery or hardware store to buy your seeds and/or seedlings. Consider what type of plants you want to grow: vegetables, fruits, herbs, and/or flowers.

- Don't feel like you need to plant the whole garden in one afternoon. The point is to have a fun date.

- Read the seed packaging or look on the web to find out the needs of your plant: Does it need lots of direct sunlight, or does it prefer shade or half shade/half sun? What about water and fertilizer?

- Pick the best spot for your plant or garden, and consider adding a little fertilizer or compost.

Talking Points

- What did it feel like to get your hands dirty?

- Depending on where you decide to plant your seeds, you may need to do some weeding along the way. What are the "weeds" in your life or marriage that make it hard for you to grow in the ways you desire?

- In what areas would you like to grow this year? Does each of you have one or two personal goals?

- Which of the following plant types best describes what you desire for your relationship?

  Vegetable—I want a relationship that is healthy and helps us become better people.

  Fruit—I want our relationship to be sweet and enjoyable.

  Flower—I want our relationship to be a beautiful thing that impacts others around us.

  Herb—I want a relationship that is spicy and makes life interesting.

Great Date Takeaway

Like plants, relationships need to be nurtured in order to thrive. What are some ways you could nurture your relationship to keep it growing and thriving? It could be that you're thirsty for more time together, more fun, or more relationship skills. What are some weeds that might pop up that could threaten your relational health: stress, distractions, unresolved issues, or regrets? At times, some couples need outside help from an "expert gardener," such as a counselor, mentor, or coach. Have fun watching your little seeds grow this summer, and let them be a symbol of intentionally growing your marriage.

Fun in the Water
Great Date

Heather and I (Peter) grew up in Minnesota, also known as the Land of 10,000 Lakes, so we tend to think there are countless ways to have fun in, on, or around the water. On this date, you'll have the chance to enjoy the water as you boost the fun level in your relationship.

The Idea

The options for this date will be influenced by where you live and your readiness for adventure, but the common theme is water! Whether you want to go swimming or canoeing, or just sit on the shore and enjoy the view, being in and around water is fun and often free. Think about the last time you sat by a public pool. If there were any children in the pool, you may have noticed their inexhaustible energy for swimming and playing in the water. When was the last time you went swimming or fishing, or paddled a canoe? Remember what it felt like to do a cannonball off the diving board? Perhaps you have fond memories of wading in the water and collecting shells. Maybe you know how to surf, snorkel, or sail, and it's time to dust off that old equipment and use it. It doesn't matter if

you live near the ocean, a lake, a river, or a pool; it's time to get in touch with that inner child and have some inexpensive fun together.

Before Your Date

- Discuss your options and make a plan that sounds like fun for both of you.

- Consider the level of adventure you want to pursue. This could range from wakeboarding to surfing, swimming, or wading. Some couples may simply decide to go for a walk along the shore. Decide what sounds like the best fit for the two of you.

- Ideas to consider: swim, wade, canoe, fish, boat, water-ski, dive, snorkel, surf, sail, jet-ski, stroll on the beach . . .

On Your Date

- Be safe! If you don't know how to swim, don't feel any pressure to go into the water; just enjoy the view.

- Remember your budget and don't feel the need to buy new water equipment. If you have some water toys or can borrow some from friends, go ahead and use them.

- Depending on where you live, you might have to pay for parking or water access.

Talking Points

- At what age did you learn to swim? What was that experience like?

- What's the most fun you've ever had with a water activity?

- Is there any water activity (sailing, snorkeling, etc.) you've never done that you'd like to try?

- Why do you think so many adults and couples stop pursuing fun activities in their lives?

- On a scale from 1 (low fun) to 10 (high fun), how "fun" is your life these days?

- What is something you could do together to boost your fun level?

Great Date Takeaway

Life often demands that we establish routines and schedules to remain effective, but our relationships don't need to fall into mundane patterns lacking fun or adventure. After almost twenty years of marriage, Heather and I (Peter) went snorkeling for the first time this year. We were able to borrow some equipment and venture out into the ocean. Heather had never been snorkeling before, and I was sorry it took us so long to try this experience together. There are no excuses for letting a marriage become stuck in a boring routine. All it takes to liven things up is some creativity energy. We want our marriage to include a lifelong pursuit of fun and learning that we share together as a couple. We hope this Fun in the Water Date has helped you reconnect with some fun and identify potential future adventures you can pursue together.

Farmers Market
Great Date

When Peter and I (Heather) lived in California, we regularly had a Saturday morning Farmers Market Date. One tradition at the market was to pick up a large bag of oranges that would provide enough citrus to make fresh juice each morning until the next Saturday. The price of the bag of oranges cost less than a carton of orange juice from the grocery store! Today, many communities hold weekly farmers markets. Find one near you and make it a date!

The Idea

Farmers markets make a great setting for a date on a budget. You will find local farmers selling a variety of flowers and produce, breads, cheese, honey, and meats. Often you will have a chance to sample a number of new flavors. Some stands may even offer specialty foods such as pesto, roasted nuts, or homemade pies.

Before Your Date

- Look online or in the local newspapers to find a farmers market near you.

- Farmers markets are usually held weekly. Find a market you want to check out, or go to one you've enjoyed in the past.

- Dress for the weather and wear comfortable shoes.

- You may want to bring your camera to capture the colors of the flowers and produce.

- Bring your own bags or a basket.

On Your Date

- Stick to your budget for the market.

- Wander the aisles together looking for fun and creative ways to spend your money. You'll be sure to find some fresh produce or flowers to enjoy.

- Try something new. Many stands offer samples.

- Talk with the merchants and farmers. They usually have stories to tell about the things they have brought to sell. Often you can get gardening or cooking tips from them as well.

- Find a place to relax and watch other people at the market.

- Take time finding the best bang for your buck. Usually similar items are priced differently from one stand to another.

Talking Points

- What new things did you see or discover at the market?

- Did you pick up any tips that you would like to try with your own garden or cooking?

- What was your favorite food you found at the market?

- How do you feel about the way you spent your $10?

Great Date Takeaway

When arriving at the market, it is easy to get caught up in the scene and buy something from the first stand you see. Being patient and taking your time gives you an opportunity to see more and possibly make better choices. In our microwave-paced culture, it is good to slow down and consider all of your options before making a quick impulse buy. A farmers market is an ideal setting to relax and slow down. Have fun!

Apple Picking
Great Date

Nothing tastes better than a fresh apple picked right from the tree! Just ask Claudia. She grew up in Ellijay, Georgia, where her dad was an apple grower. Each summer she worked in her dad's apple house packing apples. After we started dating, I (Dave) spent one summer working for Claudia's dad in the apple orchards picking apples, so you might say this date is dear to our hearts—it's part of our history.

The Idea

Most children today don't have the luxury of picking apples right off the tree. Actually, not many adults have had that experience either, so picking apples can be a fun date. Many orchards offer the option of picking your own fruit. You'll be amazed how many apples you can buy for $10 if you pick them yourself.

Before Your Date

- Check out apple orchards in your area.
- If you don't live in apple country, research what other fruits or crops (strawberries, peaches, pumpkins) are the "pick your own" variety.

- Another option is to find fields of flowers where the same principle applies. Picking your own flowers is cheaper than buying them at a florist or grocery store.

On Your Date

- Wear comfortable clothes and shoes. This date may require a lot of stretching and reaching. Sometimes the best fruit is the hardest to reach.

- This might be one date where you make an exception and bring the kids along. Family memories can also enrich your marriage.

Talking Points

- What is your favorite variety of apples?
- Do you have a favorite fruit?
- What childhood memories do you have of picking fruit or flowers?
- Share which flowers are your favorites.

Great Date Takeaway

As you enjoyed picking apples together, did you consider the work involved in cultivating and maintaining an apple orchard? Having a successful orchard requires more skill and hard work than one might think. It is also work to cultivate fruit in your marriage. What are the fruits you would desire to experience more of in your relationship? The apostle Paul encouraged the Galatians to desire the fruits of the Spirit: love, joy, peace, forbearance (patience), kindness, goodness, faithfulness, gentleness and self-control.[10] What would your marriage look like if these fruits were cultivated in your life? You might be the "apple" of each other's eye.

Snow Hike
Great Date

We know not everyone reading this book lives where there is snow, so this could also be a Sand Hike Great Date. For us (the Arps), snow days are rare, so when the flakes start falling, it's time for our Snow Hike Date. Fresh snow puts a magical spin on our world, and great conversations just seem to follow as we take the time to enjoy the softly falling flakes. It's fun to forge our own path and see our footprints in the snow. Who knows who might follow our path.

The Idea

Bundle up and head outdoors. Walk around your neighborhood or in a nearby park. Be a child again and have a snowball fight. When you return home, enjoy large mugs of hot chocolate.

Before Your Date

- Grab scarves, hats, gloves, and a waterproof jacket. Once Claudia wore her down jacket, only to find out it wasn't waterproof and that wet down is neither warm nor comfortable.
- Take along water and energy bars.
- Be sure to take your camera or smartphone.

On Your Date

- Enjoy being outside in the snow. If the snow is light and fluffy, lie down and make snow angels.

- Use a walking app just in case you get lost so you can find your way back home. See our Take a Hike (Together) Great Date #20.

- When you return home, if you still have lots of energy, grab two snow shovels and shovel your driveway or sidewalk. You could also shovel your elderly neighbor's walkway. See our Volunteer Date #30 for more ideas to bless others!

Talking Points

- How open are you to being spontaneous when the weather changes?

- Who have been your mentors? Who could you mentor?

- What do you think about exploring new paths?

- How important is the "fun factor" in your relationship?

Great Date Takeaway

When you take the time to walk together in the snow, you will have a new appreciation for the beautiful world God created. Think about the times when you were willing to forge new paths that enhanced your relationship. Looking ahead, affirm your willingness to keep exploring new pathways. Seize the moment. Depending on where you live, the snow might be gone tomorrow. Seize the time now to build your marriage today.

45

Holiday Workout
Great Date

Dave and I (Claudia) hate to admit it, but the weeks surrounding Thanksgiving and Christmas are when we tend to neglect each other, eat too much, and exercise the least—all of which leaves us feeling stressed and disconnected. We're so busy preparing for the holidays that it's easy to forget our dating habit. I tend to overdo the decorating and baking (sugar cookies and gingerbread men, candies, cakes, and other goodies). Ahhh! Can't you just see the carbs going on! So I suggested planning a few Holiday Workout Dates to keep us sane, healthy, and connected. Maybe you'll want to join us this year.

The Idea

Few people diet during the holidays. Quite the contrary, the typical person takes on an extra five to ten pounds by the New Year. Who wants to do that? We don't, and you probably don't either. So why not be proactive and plan several Holiday Workout dates? Fitness dating can help you take good care of yourself and your marriage while you are also taking control of some of those extra calories.

Before Your Date

- You may want to come up with several Holiday Workout Dates you can have between Thanksgiving and Christmas. Here are a couple of suggestions to get you started.

  Visit a health club. Many health clubs, aerobics programs, and fitness centers offer trial memberships or guest passes. Pick up a couple of them and head to the club.

  Work out together at home. You can also use workout DVDs and have your date at home. Search for "workout DVD" on the Internet and you'll find hundreds of free videos or DVDs with exercise routines and advice.

  Fitness-walk mini-dates. Take a 15- to 30-minute walk together each evening after dinner. Commit to walking together each day between now and Christmas. It's a great time to check in with each other and to stay connected.

On Your Date

- Find what appeals to you and choose from the suggestions above. Life is busy, but stick to your plan.

- If you want to work out together at home, but you don't have the equipment, try using exercise bands. They are inexpensive, and they are also good to take along when you are traveling.

- You can do modified push-ups by pushing against your kitchen counter and modified squats using a chair.

- Be creative. The turkey and dressing and pumpkin pie will taste so much better when you know you've done your due diligence!

Talking Points

- How did it feel to work out together?

- Are you a walker? Sprinter? Jogger? (See Find Our Pace Great Date #24.)

- What is your favorite calorie-burning activity?
- Do you have a favorite high-calorie holiday dish? (It could be a reward for your Workout Dates.)
- What would you say are your strengths as a couple?
- Is there something you could do between Thanksgiving and Christmas to strengthen your marriage?

Great Date Takeaway

We hope you will have fun as you work out, exercise, and walk together. We also hope you will enjoy more energy during the holidays and that eating some of your favorite Thanksgiving and Christmas dishes this year will be guilt-free. Take some time to reflect on the true meaning of Christmas. And as you start the New Year, remember that just as you need to exercise and keep your body healthy, you need to work at keeping your marriage relationship healthy too. Keep exercising those marriage muscles by talking, encouraging each other, working through issues, and having fun together.

Christmas Lights
Great Date

Each year in communities across the country, homeowners spend time, money, and energy decorating the exterior of their homes for the holidays. Heather loves to get the Christmas decorations up right after Thanksgiving. And of course she wants me (Peter) to hang the outdoor lights across the front of our house (not my favorite job). If you're like me, maybe you need a little inspiration from others who are decorating this year. This Christmas Lights Date provides a low-key opportunity to enjoy the sights, sounds, and memories of the holiday, and it may be just the motivation you need.

The Idea

Tour nearby neighborhoods and enjoy the Christmas lights. You don't have to look far to find great light displays, green garlands, intricate nativity scenes, and whimsical yard ornaments. Add to this the fact that many radio stations switch their programming to classic holiday music, and you've got a ready-made holiday tour just waiting for you. Many communities have official tree-lighting events that involve additional fun activities. Another idea is to wander through seasonal Christmas-themed markets. These sights

and sounds set the tone to be sentimental as you reminisce about past holiday memories. Because the holidays are often associated with family, you'll have a chance to talk about your families of origin as well. On this date, try to learn something new about your spouse's family traditions.

Before Your Date

- Keep your eyes open in the days leading up to your date so you have in mind the streets where homeowners have put some time and energy into their displays.
- Plan on spending a couple of hours on this date.
- Other than gas money, this date is sure to come in under your $10 budget. Pack something to drink and some snacks.

On Your Date

- Tune in to a good radio station or bring along your own favorite recorded holiday music. Try to find favorite songs from your past as well.
- If you live in a cold climate, add some hot chocolate or warm apple cider to your traveling holiday home tour.
- If the weather is mild or you live in a warmer climate, you may want to walk or bike your tour instead.
- Park the car afterward and talk about your date and the variety of decorations you enjoyed. What were your favorite light displays?
- If it is very cold outside, you might want to stop somewhere for coffee or hot chocolate, or go home and enjoy a hot drink by the fire while you talk about your date.

Talking Points

- Do you prefer classic decorations or something more on the whimsical side?
- What is your favorite holiday song?
- What traditions did your family typically observe over the holidays? (Consider decorations, special foods, annual gatherings, rituals, and religious observances.)
- Share a couple of your most vivid holiday memories from your childhood.
- What do you find stressful and/or enjoyable about the holidays now?
- What would you like more of/less of this holiday season?

Great Date Takeaway

In the hustle and bustle of the holidays, it's easy to miss enjoying the sights and sounds of the Christmas season. Just as you took time to enjoy the Christmas Lights Date, look for other ways to slow down and together enjoy this special time of the year. Maybe you learned something new about your spouse's past. It is never too late for discovery and new levels of understanding. Perhaps you remembered some aspect of the holidays of your childhood that you'd like to be more intentional about integrating into your current celebrations. Look for more opportunities to enjoy reminiscing or reconnecting with the reason for the season. Whatever your takeaway, we hope you had a chance to connect as a couple as you enjoyed the holiday sights and sounds.

Unique and Unusual
GREAT DATES

47

Solid Gold
Great Date

A $10 Solid Gold Date sounds like an oxymoron. But not so fast—it may be a fun date and a unique way to fund a number of future dates. A recent trip to the dentist definitely cost more than $10, but it led to a fun way to "fund" future dates for Dave and me (Claudia). No one likes to hear "That filling has to go. You need a crown." But the good news is the fillings that needed replacing were gold. (I know, I'm revealing my age here.) The dental assistant had gone through the same process and gave me this suggestion: "You can sell your gold fillings and any other gold you might have around the house, like jewelry that is broken or jewelry you just don't like or use anymore." Inspired, I went home and began searching for gold, thus leading to our Solid Gold Date. You might want to do the same.

The Idea

Have a gold scavenger hunt! Look through your junk drawers and jewelry box and collect any gold jewelry you no longer wear or want. (Don't overlook gold fillings you may have replaced.) And what about that broken gold chain that you will never get around to repairing and wouldn't wear if you did? You can sell your unwanted

gold and silver and make enough money for several great dates. We did, and it amounted to several hundred dollars!

Before Your Date

- Look through your jewelry and see what you can find. Pull out what you no longer want or probably won't wear again.
- Most gold dealers will also buy silver, so include any silver pieces you no longer want or need.
- Search online for gold dealers in your area and check them out. Research the going price for an ounce of gold.

On Your Date

- Double-check with each other to make sure you're not selling a family heirloom or something that is precious to the other person.
- After exchanging your gold for dollars, stop off for a milk shake or favorite coffee.

Talking Points

- What are your best "golden memories"?
- How would you like to spend the cash you received in exchange for your gold and silver?
- What future dates would you like to have that this date might fund? Maybe even a weekend getaway?
- What else might you sell to provide extra spending cash?

Great Date Takeaway

Just as you looked through your home and identified broken jewelry or items you no longer wanted or needed, think about what in your life might also need to go in order to have a Solid Gold marriage. Is there anything you could give up or make a lower priority that would release resources such as time and energy to invest in your marriage? Look for small blocks of time to sit and talk with each other. Remember the proverb "A word fitly spoken is like apples of gold in a setting of silver."[11] You can add more "gold" to your marriage just by adding words of encouragement and praise for each other!

Romantic Dinner at Nine
Great Date

Because Dave and I (Claudia) are often on the road and eat out a lot, one of our favorite dates is making do with what food we have at home and turning it into a late Romantic Dinner Date. We love the thought of a good meal that has already been paid for—we just have to shop at home to find it.

The Idea

The idea of this date is to "shop at home" for a romantic dinner for two. No need to head to an expensive restaurant, and you don't have to text for takeout. Just visit your "home market." You may be amazed at what you can find hidden in the back of your pantry, freezer, or refrigerator. Then have fun preparing and eating it together. Take your time. Consider having a 9:00 pm seating for your romantic dinner. This will give you time to leisurely prepare the meal and get the kids settled before your reservation.

Before Your Date

Look through your pantry, refrigerator, and freezer to ensure there are indeed some treasures you can turn into a romantic meal.

Pull out your best dishes and set a romantic table for two with candles and music. If your children are old enough to be up, let them help you set the table. Kids love to see their parents setting aside time to be romantic, even if they pretend to be grossed out.

On Your Date

From food you discovered at your home market, plan your menu. Here are some items you might find.

Appetizers

Some suggestions are crackers, cheese, nuts, fruit, or raw vegetables. Use salad dressing for dipping. Bread dipped in olive oil is also a good appetizer. (Did you know that restaurants serve bread as an appetizer because it whets your appetite so you will order more food?) Prepare your appetizers and enjoy eating them together while preparing your main course.

Main Course

While it may be challenging to come up with a main course without a trip to the grocery store, think outside the box. Mac and cheese? (We always have it on hand for the grandkids. It's the go-to main course for our vegetarian grandson.) What about "breakfast at night" with French toast or waffles? French toast is great way to use slightly old bread. Pasta is another easy main course. You can be creative and add whatever you find to make the sauce. Turn leftovers into a grilled sandwich, quesadilla, or an omelet. Melted cheese is a favorite ingredient to spruce up leftovers! You might even strike it rich and discover two steaks in the back of the freezer. Whatever menu you choose, enjoy preparing it together knowing it's not costing an extra penny.

Dessert

Look again and see what you can find for a romantic dessert. Forget counting carbs and calories and go with your favorite easy (on-hand) dessert. Fruit dusted with cinnamon makes a great dessert, as does that chocolate bar you've been hiding or saving for a special occasion. (This is that occasion!) What about leftover Halloween or Easter candy? I just looked in our freezer and discovered leftover cookie dough from last Christmas—easy to slice and bake. These will be great with a bowl of ice cream, if Dave hasn't already eaten it. I often keep brownie or cookie mix in our pantry for a quick dessert.

Talking Points

- While you eat, talk about what makes you desire each other— what is appetizing about your relationship?

- Talk about the foundations of your relationship when you consider your main course. What are your core beliefs that keep your marriage a priority?

- During dessert, talk about the sweet, enriching qualities you admire in each other.

Great Date Takeaway

Estimate what it would have cost you to have this dinner out, then celebrate the money you saved. Maybe you want to assemble an emergency Romantic Dinner Kit to have on hand when you're just too tired to go out or when your budget says, "No way!" You'll be surprised how energizing it can be just to stay home, focus on each other, and enjoy private seating in your Romantic Restaurant for Two. Now look for ways to compliment each other this week. Give at least one honest compliment each day. Remember, man does not live by bread alone. We need food for the soul of our marriage as well.

Take a Spin
Great Date

I (Peter) have always driven practical used cars, but lately have been talking about wanting something fun and impractical (to some), like an SUV. This has surprised Heather, who thought she knew exactly what to expect from me. On this date, you'll have the chance to take a car for a free test-drive, share your dreams, and create a great memory together as a couple.

The Idea

Stop and consider what kind of car catches your eye as you drive down the road. If you dream a little bit, in what sort of automobile do you picture yourself? The idea for this date is that you'll each pick a car you find intriguing, go to a local dealer, and ask to test-drive that vehicle. It may be helpful to pick a car above your budget to alleviate any chance of buying it!

The point of this date is not to buy a new car, but to have a fun experience as you explore your dreams together. The dealership sales staff is typically very open to getting people out for a test-drive, and it is not dishonest to say, "I'm interested in this vehicle, and I would love to take one for a test-drive." You can

take the salesperson's business card and thank him or her for the opportunity.

Before Your Date

- Start thinking ahead of time about what sort of car you'd like to drive.
- Locate a dealership in your area.
- Allow enough time for each of you to test-drive a car. Unless you both choose the same brand, you'll likely need to go to two separate dealerships or turn this into two dates!
- Remember to bring your driver's license and insurance card. Some dealers require these for test-drives.
- Leave your credit information at home, especially if you're a natural spender. Salespeople can be very convincing, and you don't want to be tempted to do something you'll regret. A new car would exceed your $10 budget!

On Your Date

- Since this is only a test-drive, you can pick a totally impractical car. For some, it may be that convertible you've always wanted. Others will go for the sports car or SUV. Have fun with your selection.
- Don't judge or criticize each other's choice. Let your spouse have fun with the test-drive even if he or she chooses something that doesn't appeal to you.
- If your time is limited, decide on a single car you'd both like to test-drive. This will allow you to visit just one dealership and maximize your driving time.
- If you're not comfortable taking your dream car out for a test-drive, at least go to the dealership showroom and sit in one.

Talking Points

- What did you learn about each other's car choices? Were you surprised?

- What features did you like about the cars you tested?

- Thinking back over your lifetime, consider all the cars you (or your family) have owned. Which was your favorite (and why)?

- If you owned your dream car and could drive it anywhere, where would you go?

Great Date Takeaway

Relationships grow when you spend quality time together, create great memories, and share dreams. It's easy to assume we know everything there is to know about our spouse. This is especially true for couples who have been together for a long time. But people and preferences can change over time. Giving one another the opportunity to dream out loud is a gift that can lead to new discoveries. We trust this date will provide you with the time and space needed for a deeper level of exploration as you learn more about each other's tastes, hopes, and dreams.

Play With a Pet
Great Date

The Idea

When we (the Arps) get too old to travel, perhaps we will get a pet. Until then, we enjoy being around others' furry friends. Recently we got to know Margo and Alfred, two adorable French water dogs that are part of the Arp extended family zoo. We observed how much work they require, so the next time we yearn for a furry friend, we will have a Play With a Pet Date.

If you have a dog, you could have a dog-walking date. In many cities, you can find dog parks where your dog can romp and play freely with other dogs. It can be a fun setting for great conversations as well.

Before Your Date

If you, like us, have no pets, here are several suggestions:

- Borrow your friend's pet for the afternoon. When our sons were growing up, we used to pet-sit for long enough to know who really had to do the work of caring for them, and it wasn't

our sons. (Actually, it wasn't Claudia either.) But having a dog for an afternoon is a different story. It can actually be fun.

- Visit a pet store. We've heard of pet stores that let the cats roam the store just waiting for someone to pet them, fall in love with them, buy them, and take them home. (Since this is a $10 Great Date, don't even go there!)

- Check out your local animal shelter or Humane Society. Give them a call, as some shelters like people to come and play with the cats or walk the dogs.

On Your Date

- Enjoy sitting around and playing with the pets.

- Observe the various pets and see what lessons they might teach you about love, loyalty, and life.

- *Disclaimer:* We assume no responsibility for any furry friends that might end up going home with you.

Talking Points

- Do you presently have pets, or did you have pets growing up? If so, what was your all-time favorite pet?

- If you don't have a pet at present, would you like to have one in the future? What kind of pet would you choose?

- One trait dogs have is their unconditional love and loyalty to their owner. What does loyalty mean to you in your marriage relationship? What about unconditional love?

Great Date Takeaway

Pets can be therapeutic and good for your emotional health, but they also create stress when untrained. What can we learn from

pets that might benefit our marriage? First, it takes effort and work to train a dog, and it takes effort and work to build a successful marriage as well. A dog's wagging tail demonstrates how glad the dog is to see you and reminds us how important it is in our marriage to show up happy. Dogs also have great eye contact. Just looking into the friendly eyes of Margo and Alfred made us want to take them home with us. Instead, we took home their lessons of love and loyalty, and a reminder to keep working on our relationship.

A River Runs Through It
Great Date

Our disclaimer: This is about several high-energy dates, and they will not be for everyone! They are for the strong of heart and back, and those who love nature and gardening.

Having a "river" run through our yard was not by design—it was the result of a drainage problem. And being a bit adventuresome, we turned this challenge into a number of $10 Great Dates. The landscaping company wanted to re-grade our backyard to prevent water from collecting around our house and seeping into our basement. We could see the dollar signs going down the drain when Claudia came up with a clever solution: let's build a dry streambed and divert the water away from our house. Voila! Problem solved— and the good part was that it resulted in a number of cheap dates.

The Idea

You don't have to have a drainage problem to enjoy this date, but you do need a yard. We also had a lot of rock on our lot left over from the original owners who built our house and had added stacked stone to the entryway. Together, we chose the path for our dry streambed that was pleasing to the eye and would also divert the water away from our house. Then, together, we dug out the streambed and added rocks. On other dates, we planted ground cover and other native plants on each side of the dry streambed.

Before Your Date

Google *dry streambeds* and look at the pictures. Choose the look that suits you and the space you have.

- In deciding where you want your dry streambed, you might want to tie it in to where water comes out from your gutter system.

- Choose rocks, stones, and gravel in a variety of shapes and sizes, combining smooth river rocks with sharper-edged rocks to make it look natural.

- If you need rocks, check out local rock quarries on a Quarry Date. You can buy river rocks by the pound, and they are much cheaper than at a garden center. (*Disclaimer:* the rocks will throw you over your budget, but you may put this cost under "home improvement" instead of date night.)

- Check with neighbors who might need to get rid of extra rocks. Our neighbors had just completed a rock wall and needed the leftover rock removed. We were happy to oblige them.

- Suggested plants for naturalizing your dry streambed are pachysandra, northern sea oats, astilbe, fern, and sedum. (*Note:* This will also depend on your part of the country, so check out what grows in your region at www.davesgarden.com. *Disclaimer:* This is not my website, for sure!)

On Your Date

- Respect your back! It's easy to overdo it on this date, so we suggest making this a series of dates.

- First, decide your stream's future path. An easy way to determine where the stream will look natural and pleasing to the eye is to use a hose to outline the path to help you visualize how wide you want it, how you want it to curve, and so on. Definitely go for a meandering path rather than a straight line.

- A width to depth ratio of two to one should be about right. For instance, if your stream is four feet wide, you would want to make it about two feet deep.

- A planting shovel is ideal for establishing the edges of the streambed. For digging out the streambed, Dave prefers a regular shovel while Claudia likes to keep using her planting shovel.

- Avoid putting the rock in a pattern.

- Take plenty of water breaks. From time to time, pull up a couple of chairs and enjoy watching your dry streambed become a reality.

Talking Points

- What is your favorite landscaping style? Are your tastes similar or different?

- What are some plants that might work well with your dry streambed?

- What will you need to do to maintain your dry streambed? From time to time we have to weed ours, and in the fall we blow the leaves away.

- Talk about the character qualities of rock and how God, the Rock of Ages, is foundational for a rock-solid marriage.

Great Date Takeaway

When finished, hopefully your dry streambed will look natural and fitting for the location. How would this relate to your relationship? For instance, building a rock-solid marriage is a lot of work, but to others observing your marriage, it might appear easy to maintain. What kind of marriage maintenance is needed to keep your marriage healthy? Marriage, like gardening, requires teamwork and elbow grease. It's hard work, but well worth it!

Estate Sale
Great Date

Our friends Greg and Becky visit estate sales not only as a great date but also as a side business. For years, Becky rented a small booth in an antique mall and would often buy their estate sale treasures to sell in her booth. Greg, who is not a natural-born shopper, says their Estate Sale Dates are actually fun and possible to pull off for $10 max.

The Idea

Pick a weekend for your adventure and scan the papers and Internet for estate sales in your area. Go together and split your ten bucks—five bucks each. See who can come up with the best bargain and most unique purchase.

Before Your Date

- Research estate sales in your area. Check out www.estatesales .net or type *estate sales services* into a search engine to find local firms. On their websites, you'll find information on upcoming events in your area.

- Plan your route and choose the time for your date. Estate sales usually occur on the weekends.

- Estate sales that advertise "Everything must go" tend to offer the best deals.

- Talk about what you hope to discover. Becky looks for kitchen items that sell well in her booth, and Greg loves to find unique Christmas tree ornaments.

- Pack a picnic lunch or snack and bottled water so you will stay within your budget.

On Your Date

- Wear comfortable shoes and take your own shopping bags.

- If you're looking for a special item, hit the sales early. If you're flexible and can scope out the sales on the first day (often on Thursdays or Fridays when prices are high), you can choose which ones to revisit at the end of the sale (when prices are low).

- Don't be shy about bargaining! It just might help you stay within your budget.

- If you don't find any treasures, or the price is too high, don't be afraid to walk away empty-handed.

- Be on the lookout for unique gifts for children and/or grandchildren, or a good friend or neighbor.

- Bring cash.

Talking Points

- Many estate sales are in older, larger homes with lots of character. Observe the layout of the house and what you like and don't like about it.

- If you were holding your own estate sale, what five items would you want to sell? Maybe it's time to have a de-clutter date and sale of your own!
- Did you find a favorite treasure at an estate sale?
- What do you treasure about your marriage?
- Why do you think marriage is called the "holy *estate* of marriage"?

Great Date Takeaway

While celebrating the estate sale treasure you may have found, don't neglect appreciating all the treasures you can find in the "estate of your marriage." The wedding ceremony from the *Anglican Book of Common Prayer* from 1662 (which has remained little changed today), proclaims holy matrimony to be an "honorable estate," instituted by God. Did you realize that Jesus performed the first miracle at a wedding in Cana? Weddings are great celebrations, but after the wedding comes the marriage, when you have the opportunity to live out this holy estate by loving, comforting, honoring, and keeping each other in sickness and in health, forsaking all others as long as you both shall live. Why not take some time today to reaffirm your vows and treasure each other?

Cheap Child Care Options

One of the quickest ways to add expense to your great dates is the cost of babysitters. However, we don't want child care to be the obstacle that keeps you from enjoying quality time in your marriage. Here are some creative and cheap options for child care.

- *Do a daytime date.* When our kids became school-aged, Peter and I (Heather) found that lunchtime dates were a great option because they didn't require a babysitter. It also allowed us to find less expensive menu options, and we were able to enjoy more daylight hours together.

- *Recruit relatives.* Find a relative or grandparent who would be happy to spend time with your kids. Offer to have them over for a meal or do something to show your appreciation for the gift of their time.

- *Adopt grandparents* if your parents live far away. Dave and Claudia had an older couple who volunteered to be "stand- in" grandparents for them.

- *Trading places.* Find a family with kids and plan a weekly date "swap." One week you take their kids, and another they take yours.

- *Use the "At-Home Great Dates" section* of this book and have dates at home while the kids are sleeping or otherwise occupied. A little dose of the "electric babysitter" (TV) can be a great investment in your marriage and family. One father said he began to feel amorous whenever he heard the theme song from *The Lion King*.

- *Parent Night Out programs.* Many communities and churches host Parent Night Out events, making child care more affordable for parents and a fun option for kids to look forward to instead of feeling left behind.

- *Take advantage of the busyness.* You may find as your kids get older and you are running them to lessons, practices, and friends' homes, you have an opening for you and your spouse to slip in a date!

- *Sleepover date.* Do your children ever have sleepovers on the same night? Lucky you! You can have an entire evening and morning together. Try coordinating this with another family and reciprocate the favor for them!

When our kids were young, they would sometimes fuss when we were heading out on a date and leaving them behind with Grandma or a sitter. We would explain to them the importance of our having Mommy and Daddy time. It wasn't long before they began to see divorce in some of the families around them. They understood a bit more the value of our taking the time to nurture our marriage. You may have heard the saying "The greatest gift you can give your children is a strong marriage." Don't use the kids as an excuse not to take time for dating. Instead, they can be one of your strongest motivators!

Acknowledgments

We are grateful to our friends, family, and participants in our 10 Great Dates Seminars who shared their creative dates with us so we could pass them on to you.

Special thanks to Tim Peterson, Jeff Braun, Nancy Renich, LaVonne Downing, Hannah Carpenter, and the rest of the team at Bethany House Publishers who make writing fun for us.

Thank you, Greg Johnson, not only for representing us—which you do so well—but also for contributing one of your own fun $10 Great Dates.

Notes

1. Philippians 4:8
2. Proverbs 24:3
3. Ephesians 4:26
4. Proverbs 15:13 (NLT)
5. Colossians 3:13
6. Hebrews 12:1
7. Proverbs 17:22 (ESV)
8. Acts 20:35
9. Ecclesiastes 4:9
10. Galatians 5:22–23
11. Proverbs 25:11 (ESV)

About the Authors

Peter J. Larson, PhD, is a licensed clinical psychologist and currently serves as the Marriage and Family Initiative Lead at Gloo, Inc. He is the coauthor of the PREPARE/ENRICH Customized Version and the Couple Checkup Inventory and book. **Heather Larson**, MS, has her master's degree in psychology. She is the founder of Bridgewell Coaching and works as a Christian relationship coach. She and Peter regularly teach and speak together. They are the hosts of the *10 Great Dates Before You Say "I Do"* DVD curriculum. The Larsons have been married for twenty years and have three children.

Claudia Arp and **David Arp**, MSW, are founders of Marriage Alive International, a ground-breaking ministry dedicated to providing resources and training to empower churches to help build better marriages. The Arps are authors of numerous books and video curricula, including the *10 Great Dates* series and the Gold Medallion Award–winning *The Second Half of Marriage*. The Arps have appeared on the NBC *Today Show,* CBS *This Morning,* PBS, and *Focus on the Family*. Their work has been featured in publications such as *USA Today*, the *Washington Post, New York Times, Wall Street Journal*, and *Time* magazine. When they are not writing or speaking, you'll probably find them hiking trails in northern Virginia, where they live, or in the Austrian Alps, where they love to hike.

More Great Dates

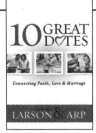

While juggling the kids, work, church, and community commitments, are you and your spouse finding time to connect? When was the last time you had a good talk about faith or did a devotional together?

To help you jump-start deeper connections, four marriage experts have come up with ten creative date ideas, each centered on a spiritual theme, including:
- Appreciating your differences
- Experiencing God together
- Facing the storms of life
- Connecting through prayer

With the planning taken care of—including flexible suggestions for before, during, and after the date— you and your spouse can simply enjoy the time sharing what's important in life.

Download a free leader's guide for small groups at 10greatdates.org.

eat Dates: Connecting Faith, Love, and Marriage
:er and Heather Larson & David and Claudia Arp

◈ BETHANYHOUSE

 Stay up-to-date on your favorite books and authors with our free e-newsletters. Sign up today at bethanyhouse.com.

 Find us on Facebook. facebook.com/BHPnonfiction

 Follow us on Twitter. @bethany_house